The Truth Shall Set You Free: THE PRISON LETTERS

Dawn Densmore-Parent

Dedication

To my friend 'SueBee':

"Thank you for your encouragement, help and support for my vision. There is rarely a day that goes by that you are not thought of by those of us here on earth.

I look forward to seeing you on the other side, my friend! In the meantime, please tell Jesus I said "Hi!"

"Surely I come quickly".
"Amen, even so, come, Lord Jesus"
Revelation 22: 20

My Thanks

My deepest gratitude and thanks to those who are included in this book, as well as to those who encouraged and supported me during the process of writing with thoughtful feedback.

My thanks especially to Fabien Parent for his love and care for me and my family! My thanks also to my family members, who daily inspire me and help me to 'want to 'do' and 'be' my very best each day!

Cover Design by: Tamara Smith, UVM Print and Mail, VT

Scriptures are from the Holy Bible, King James Version

©Copyright 2021

ISBN: 978-1-7342353-3-3

INTRODUCTION

Serving God has blessings for believers right now, as well as eternal rewards.

For I know the thoughts that I think toward you, saith the Lord, thoughts of peace, and not of evil, to give you an expected end (Jeremiah 29:11).

When we walk in love towards God and one another we create a foundation for the Lord to reveal Himself to us in extraordinary ways.

And ye shall seek me, and find me, when ye shall search for me **with all your heart** (Jeremiah 29:13).

Contents

Chapter 1 — Every Life Matters: January Letters 7

Chapter 2 — The Tapestry: The February Letters 23

Chapter 3 — The Bridge Builder: The March Letters 35

Chapter 4 — Above the Maze: The April Letters 45

Chapter 5 — Bear Ye Another's Burdens – The May Letters 55

Chapter 6 — Yesterday: The June Letters 69

Chapter 7 — Today: Be an Eagle! The July Letters... 77

Chapter 8 — Forever: The Rubric Cube: The August Letters 89

Chapter 9 — FAITH Waits: The September Letters... 101

Chapter 10 — Let Good Overcome Evil: The October Letters 111

Chapter 11 — Spiders and Bees: The November Letters.. 123

Chapter 12 — The Choice: The December Letters.. 133

Chapter 1

Every Life Matters: January Letters

The very hairs of your head are all numbered.

Matthew 10:30

The greatest fear for those who are in prison is that life is going on without them and that they have been forgotten. These circumstances can diminish feelings of worth, but the Lord confirms otherwise. Each of us matters so much that God actually took time to count each hair on our head. I took time one day to actually count the number of hairs that were on my hairbrush. I counted 49 hairs and thought to myself; at that rate, it is amazing I am not totally bald!

The Bible gives the account of Joseph who was betrayed by his brothers, sold into slavery, falsely accused with the result of being put in prison for many years. The events of his life certainly appeared to be 'out of God's control', but his life was in God's perfect control. Joseph's circumstances created a framework for God to refine his character in preparation for the work he would be asked to do to deliver his people and the nation of Egypt from a severe seven-year famine. Joseph had knowledge of God's Word and he had been given dreams by God, and both of these sustained him and allowed him to trust God, despite his circumstances. During this time, Joseph suffered at the hands of evil men. Those who are to be used by the Lord, often endure severe trials before their appointed purpose begins. Jesus also suffered at the hands of evil men. God does allow suffering to occur for His purposes. Joseph served God even while in prison, and God raised Jesus from the dead three days after he was crucified on a cross. The worst of times contain within them divine purpose. Believers are instructed to have faith wherever they are located, whatever the circumstances. John the Baptist, Peter and Paul all found themselves behind bars. Knowing and believing in the promises of God, accepting the GIFT of eternal life through Jesus Christ enables our mind and heart to see things from a higher point of view. God is able to set us 'free' to love others even in the midst of hatred and scorn. He empowers us through His Holy Spirit to be kind even to those who persecute us. God's purpose is to work evil for good. When we find ourselves in uncomfortable situations, the question that we need to ask is not "Why?" The question we need to ask is "What?" "What, Lord, exactly are you trying to TEACH me in this situation?" Then, we are to read the Bible and pray to the Lord to help find an answer to that question. God works His changes in us from the *'inside-out'* not from the *'outside-in'*.

"But I say to you, love your enemies, bless those who curse you, do good to those who hate you, and pray for those who spitefully use you and persecute you, that you may be sons of your Father in heaven; for He makes His sun rise on the evil and on the good, and sends rain on the just and on the unjust" (Matthew 44-45).

"Bless them that curse you, and pray for them which despitefully use you" (Luke 6:28).

THE JANUARY LETTERS

January 2, 2020   Dear (Name)

Our new kitten Grady has gotten large enough to escape a few times outside into the snow. He can RUN, and is hard to CATCH! We have decided that we cannot open the outside door without locating him and picking him up, and carrying him out with us and then depositing him back inside the door as we close it quickly. That is because he is such an escape artist! He is still capturing our hearts as he explores his new world and claims territory. He is now brave enough to go up the spiral stair case in the middle of our home. He can only do the first 3 steps. They are open stairs, so he gets scared when he looks down and then turns around, but that won't always be the case! And there is the upstairs which is an entire new level for him to investigate. So, we are working to make sure we shut our upper door at the top of the stairs.

Fabien and I went sledding yesterday on hills around our home. We made it a family affair. We had several toboggan sleds as well as coasters. The coasters spin and turn as they go down the hill and travel faster than the sleds. When we did two on a sled the weight load increased the speed on the sled! Not too surprising, as we are getting older, we find it is harder for us to get ourselves vertical again, once we are back at ground level. We must have looked pretty silly trying to help each other get back up! It was still fun and we plan to do it again. The last time we went sledding was on Fabien's farm hill, and that was almost 6 years ago. Like a lot of things, we talk about going but it was great to actually do it! Some of the 'not doing' is because the weather has to be good: not too cold so we can have a good time, and there needs to be enough snow for the sleds and coasters to slide! Seems having both at the same time is a challenge! On New Year's Eve there was a Passion program broadcast around the world that was held in the Mercedes Benz Stadium in Atlanta Georgia. In attendance were 65,000 young adults between 18 and 25 years old from universities representing every State in America as well as from countries around the world. The message was 'feelings are NOT faith' and "Now" yells louder; but "later' – last longer!" The culture says: 'Have a good time' but there are consequences to doing 'right now' thinking. The speaker encouraged students to be members of their local churches which create community. He emphasized that there is a 'deadness' of heart that comes from living just for money, sex, and material things: living for only one-self. This is referred to in the Bible as building a house upon 'sand'. Our focus needs to be on getting 'rooted' in the words of God from the Bible: which is bedrock – referred to as "building upon a 'rock'. What was amazing to me was that this was not a 'free' event. Each participant had to pay to attend, as well as pay travel costs and lodging costs to be there. The presenter used the past to help those attending understand that there are consequences to actions. His message was entitled, "Bunnies, Blizzards, and Trees". He spoke of when the 'dust bowl' hit the United States impacting 46 of the then 48 states. This occurrence was created when tractors plowed up the prairie-grass and planted wheat. The planted wheat did not grow 'deep enough to stabilize the dug-up soil. When the rain stopped and the winds arrived, there were blizzards of sand that created "Dust Towns". The dust traveled east as far as New York City and then went out to sea landing on ships 200 miles off shore. The dust killed the coyotes that ate the rabbits, creating an explosion of 15-30,000 jack rabbits that then travelled the countryside eating up everything that was in sight. The solution was created when F.D. Roosevelt ordered that trees be planted from Canada to Mexico as a wind break. This wind break worked to restore the plains. The presenter used a prop which was a 'wall of plywood' on the stage. He nailed nails to the board and then attempted to hang a very heavy piece of metal onto a nail. The metal frame, he said, represents an eternal 'soul'. Only when he used a heavy nail that went through a stud was the wall strong enough to hold the heavy piece of metal. He then swung the board around, to reveal a 'cross' made of 4x4's on the back. He encouraged students to anchor their soul to the free gift of salvation through Christ. He said, "Your 20's will bring you to your 30's, and your 30's to your 40's, and the 40's to your 50's! When you start to look back it will have seemed to have just 'flown by'. So, build your life on the solid rock of truth, which places God first, and others above yourself. I wonder what the impact would be if all of the students present actually 'did' as he recommended? I wonder what the impact would be if we ourselves listen and apply this message to our daily life. Jesus's message was to love God and love and care for one another. This is what connects us and makes us 'family'. Changing the world requires that we become vessels of honor for the Lord's use.

The 2020 message at Northside was about the Peace that comes from God when we actually 'pray' and seek God's will for our life. Indeed, Jesus is the Prince of Peace! He alone can help us to live in peace.

January 9, 2020 Dear (Name)

One of the messages we listened to on Sunday was about a soldier who was headed to Afghanistan. He ended up on the plane sitting next to a minister. A casual question was asked by the soldier to the man sitting next to him. The soldier asked, 'What do you do?" The minister replied, "I am a minister". The young man quickly replied emphatically, "I have no faith, I do NOT believe in God!" The minister said, "You MUST have an amazing story, would you like to tell me about it?" Tears came to his eyes, as the soldier told his life story to the minister. The soldier had witnessed a murder as a 13-year-old boy, and then was required to be a witness of what had happened. He had been the only witness. Growing up, he had no Dad or Mom. When he got a girlfriend, she got pregnant. That was when he joined the service to be able to pay support for his new son. Once he was abroad in a foreign country, he got another woman pregnant and had another son. Then he was told that one of his sons had been left with a man who had then molested his son at 2 years old. He told the minister, "That is why I do not believe in any God!" The minister suggested that he leave the army and go and take care of one of his sons. He replied, "No, I want to be a soldier because I enlisted to have the opportunity to 'kill' someone! I have so much RAGE inside of me that I have to get it out!" The minister was quiet, and prayed for the soldier. Then he told the soldier, that he knew of a man who also had a lot of rage, so much that he wanted to kill as many as he could, and he did just that! His name was Saul, and he was headed to kill some more people. But as he was going to do just that, he was knocked to the ground by a great light and by a voice. A man appeared to him, and Saul asked, "Who art thou?" The man replied, "I am Jesus whom thou art persecuting." That experience changed that man's life. The minister agreed that the soldier's life had been dreadful, but that if he did not seek the Lord, he would continue to live with the rage and anger that was within him. The soldier agreed that he did need to get rid of his rage and anger. Both departed the flight at their destination, but the minister added the soldier to his prayer list. He had his name and was able to actually write to him and to send him a Bible. This work of forgiveness is for each of us. To be a believer we must first ask the Lord to forgive us for our own anger and hatred, and then invite and allow God's Holy Spirit to come into our heart. This puts us in a position to be able to 'give' the very 'forgiveness' that we receive from God, to those we meet who have transgressed against us. When someone hurts another, there is a 'debt' that is owed by that person TO the person hurt. When we 'forgive' a person, what we actually are doing is removing 'that debt' that is owed to us, and that 'sets us free' from being bound to the hurt and the pain of the incident.

The Lord Jesus Christ was abused, beaten, cursed, spoken against, and eventually nailed to a cross. His words from that cross were, "Forgive them for they know not what they do!" Jesus was subsequently placed in a borrowed tomb, and guards were placed in front of it and the stone was sealed. On the third day, angels appeared at that tomb. When Mary and the other women came to anoint the body of Jesus, the angels announced 'He is not here, He has risen!" As Mary lingered and cried, she saw a man behind her and she asked where they had taken him. She assumed the man was the gardener. Then the man said, "Mary!" She immediately recognized the voice! It was the voice of Jesus's that she had heard speak her name many times before! Jesus then told her to go and tell the others that He was Risen. Jesus appeared for 40 days to many, and then to over 500 on the Mount of Olives, as he told everyone to: "Go and tell the good news". A cloud then descended and circled his feet and lifted him up into the clouds. Everyone stood looking up. Then two man came down in white appeal and said, "Ye men of Galilee, go and do as he has said." We are to believe, receive, and give – in that order. We don't know what happened to the soldier, but the Lord has promised that his Word will not return void. All of us are ministers for the message of love and peace to those we meet, so always be ready to give an answer for the hope that is in you.

January 17, 2020 Dear (name)

Fabien has been our "Mr. MacGyver" again this week! He made a train tunnel that initially was not high enough for both the train once on the track to pass through, and then the tunnel he created was too long for the rest of the cars to make the curve on the track. His clever idea was to cut the tunnel in two, and to add small wooden sections to make the tunnel higher. That worked perfectly! Then another friend called for help to install a new door knob. The inner locking mechanism was too large for the hole in the door frame. Fabien was able to drill out a larger opening and install the entry door knob. My friend was very thankful. Then another friend had a bureau that had a broken drawer, as well as a broken frame within the bureau itself. Fabien was able to reinforce the bottom of the drawer by adding small wooden braces to hold the frame back together. He then was successful in replacing the framework for the bureau itself to hold the drawer. It was very fussy work to make sure the drawer would slide on the sliders smoothly because the sliders had to be repaired, too. This week he is helping his youngest son with some construction at his home farm. One of my favorite things to do is to get to just 'watch' him work! My friend who needed the bureau fixed commented to me as we watched him repair that bureau, "Just how does he know what to do next?!" These are areas that neither of us have any experience or ability to know how to do the repairs needed. They are 'beyond' what we know. Fabien has an ability to just 'think things through' and figure things out as he goes. Such an amazing gift! Some people would get stalled and say, "It's broke, just throw it away!" But Fabien sees the value in reclaiming and repairing things. His other fix of a chest was done last week. He built a new top for it and added it to that broken chest. We got that chest from a friend of his. When we went to pick up a door from him for our garage, Fabien noticed there was a chest on a 'burn pile' of brush in the backyard. When he finished loading the door onto his truck, he asked about the chest. His friend replied, "It's broke – you can have it if you want it- I'm planning to burn it!" Fabien got it and loaded it on top of the door and we brought both home. Now that chest has become a new 'coffee table' for our friends living room in their new home. That chest is the 'focal point' of their living room. Seems everyone who visits loves that chest made into a table! I am glad that with the Lord, there are no throwaways.

The first of this week we got a hard rain storm here that went across the entire United States. We were spared the bulk of the rain, but Fabien's home farm had flooding in the meadows. The flooding almost came up to their hill where they store their giant round hay bales. In the fall, another rainstorm caused 2 or 3 of those large bales to float down the river. The water got so high then that Fabien's camper that was parked along the shore of the river, was totally under water. After the storm, we could see just the roof of the camper. After that second rain storm, we could see that the water had only gotten up to the entry door.

The beginning of January is the time when some Christians all around the world do a Daniel fast of 21 days. The start of the fast this year was on January 5. There have been several things that have occurred worldwide since that fast began.

Jan. 6 - Alaska Shohaidin volcano erupted 25,000 ft - 5 miles high

Jan. 7 – USA was hit with the storm that impacted the entire US with several people dying in the storm

Jan. 9 - Mexico Mt. Popocatepetl erupted – went 4 miles into the sky

And Peru Sabancaya volcano went 24,000 ft almost 5 miles

Jan 12 - The Philippines Taal Volcano shot 10-15 kilometers 6-9 miles

Jan 11 -Puerto Rico quake hit at 8:45 am at 5.9 after experiencing over 100 earthquakes since 1/1/20

There is a promise of the Lord that when we fast, pray and praise Him, it is like a three-fold cord that is not easily broken. These events coincided with this fast. Sadly, oftentimes, it is when people have the greatest need, that they become open to prayer and turning to God.

January 24, 2020 Dear (name)

The snow has kept us busy this week – we got a total of 12 inches but it came in spurts which required us to shovel and plow almost every day. It has been below zero as well. Audrey's entry door jammed due to the concrete foundation shifting with the freeze. Fabien removed the door and took off some of the top of the door and then reinstalled it. That fixed the problem. Our neighbor Virginia has 2 roosters, and one rooster has now taken up roosting in Audrey's garage. We have coy dog tracks around, and they can be heard at night. The rooster doesn't seem to understand when it crows at night, he is telling every predator that is in our area exactly where he is located! We are unsure how long he will be able to survive. Audrey's attempts to get the rooster to come into her chicken coop have been refused. Sadly, the rooster won't return to his home coop across the street either, because the other rooster is beating him up. The only other plan is to attempt to catch him and bring him to a new home where there is no other competing rooster.

John's baby turkeys that were hatched by the chicken that survived were: 1 male and 1 female. The Tom Turkey father has continued to be aggressive and he chases everyone that comes into their yard. John doesn't want those who visit their home to be chased by that turkey. It is pretty likely that that Tom Turkey will become dinner sometime in the future.

Hard to believe we are almost thru January. We have our respite person this coming weekend.

Fabien's youngest son has used some of the old French door windows that Fabien brought to our home when he came in 2015. He placed 3 of them sideways in the wall in his sugarhouse. It is such a wonderful use for them. These windows allow him to be able to have a work area that he can heat for the R/O machines that remove the water from the sap. The windows also allow him to see the sugar rig from that work area. Pretty soon, everyone will be tapping here in VT for sap!

Fabien's second son Chris is making 'river' tables. They are large 6-foot tables that have a 'river' flowing down the middle of the table. He fills a middle cavity with epoxy- glue that looks like 'water'. He has sold one already. The other tables he is creating look like they have a 'tree trunk' for a base – like a pedestal table – but the wood looks like a tree trunk. These also are just amazing and for us an answered prayer. We continue to pray for him to not be discouraged with 'now' VS 'before'.

The most wonderful revelation that the Lord has given me is that this earthly life does not provide us with 'true rest'. This is a rest that is different than when we are' not doing' anything. It is God that gives us the 'energy' for the moment of activity or 'task'. When we walk with the Lord's Holy spirit, amazingly at the end of a day, there is a sweet spiritual 'rest' which passes all understanding – and this opens a door for us to give Him our thanks and praise! Truly it is 'not' by might, nor by 'power', but by my Spirit, saith the Lord' that His will is done on earth. (Zechariah 4:6).

Each day it is important for us to remember that 'life' is not supposed to be 'easy' on earth. Earth is a proving ground for our eternal souls. Somehow, understanding there is a purpose to trials that come helps me get 'through' without having to have an answer for 'why' they are allowed. The Lord has promised rewards in eternity (which is forever). Ours is to have FAITH, pray, wait, and continue to go to Him for help in time of need. I have read that in eternity our entire life will appear as just one 'rainy day'.

January 31, 2020   Dear (name)

We have had our very first 'curiosity almost killed the cat' moment. Grady got under the freezer door when Audrey had the door open. Then she realized he was missing! As she looked for the cat, she realized the last place she saw him was next to her feet at her freezer door. She decided to go back and open the door. Yup! There was 'Grady' looking back up at her from inside the freezer! She said he looked bewildered and felt a little cold when she picked him up, but he was OKAY! He was in the freezer for about 1 minute. Fabien joked, "Well, we almost had a 'cat-sicle'! We all are truly relieved she found him! Seems our 'rescued cat' continues to need rescuing!

As I reflected on all of this, I could not help but realize that we are all truly like 'Grady'. Our desire to understand leads us to 'investigate' and desire to be involved with just everything around us. Our spiritual enemy uses our very own 'curiosity' against us! We should be more 'curious' about the word of God, and seek to know the Lord and follow Him, rather than chasing after the lures of this temporary world around us, seeking 'this' and then 'that'. Rather we need to seek the Lord first and be about His business. Audrey, just like the Lord and His Holy Spirit, came to Grady's rescue. The Lord's Holy spirit also comes to our rescue to help us get 'out of' the messes that we get ourselves into when we choose to live apart from living to 'please God'. Like Grady, we don't have any concept of the dangers to our eternal soul, while we are here on earth. We are 'foreigners' to the things that this earth offers: its entertainment and distractions of 'things' can draw us into 'traps' with promises of 'fulfillment' but in truth these can rob us of the riches and blessings of the treasures of fellowship with God and with one another. We gain God's blessings when we abide in His presence through meditating on key promise scriptures. It is important during the day, to ask Him how we can apply them to our life. My bible verse today was, "Shew me the path of life, in Thy presence **IS FULLNESS OF JOY!** (Psalm 16:11).

This verse revealed the 'path' my own life has taken, and of all the twists and turns, and times when I have gone backward, rather than forward, into places like the 'freezer' that have almost 'froze' any desire for the Lord. But indeed, "The Lord is good! He is a refuge in times of trouble and He cares for those who trust in Him" (Nahum 1:7).

In the book "A Shepherd Looks at Psalm 23" by W. Phillip Keller, a shepherd writes how his sheep continually got out of the fences seeking better grass than in the field he placed them in. The sheep can get trapped in fences, and can even got turned onto their back. When they are on their back, they are unable to get back up. They can die, if they are not found and turned back on their feet.

The purpose of a 'redeemed life' for those who trust in Jesus who came, died, and rose from the grave (who will return to establish His Kingdom on earth) is to BE overcomers. This is possible for us when we listen and hear and obey the Shepherd's voice. Keller told of one of his favorite sheep that he had to put down. That sheep was determined to get out of every pasture it was put into and when that sheep started leading the other sheep to do the same, he reluctantly put her down.

When we get to the other side in eternity, we will be amazed at how many times 'angels' have helped us! The Lord does allow us to exercise our 'free will choice' here on earth just like that sheep! May we seek His grace and mercy and may the Lord intervene and care for each of us.

My hymn today was: "Stand up, Stand up for Jesus! The strife will not be long, put on the gospel armor, each piece put on with prayer, to him that over cometh a crown of life shall be!"

We are to "be strong and of good courage" (Joshua 1:5&6).
"Yeh, I shall not forget thee" (Isaiah 49:15).

Chapter 2

The Tapestry: The February Letters

And after the earthquake a fire, but the Lord was not in the fire, and after the fire, a still small voice.

1 Kings 19:12

Our life is very much like a tapestry. The poem, "The Weaver" provides encouragement that 'the dark threads are as needful in the weaver's skillful plan, as the threads of gold and silver in the pattern He has planned." The problem is that we view life typically from a 'horizontal' perspective only. From that viewpoint, life truly will make very little sense. It is only when we incorporate FAITH in a God who created all things for His purpose and His glory, that we are able to comprehend that there is actually a purpose in the suffering and pain that is allowed in our lives. The older we are, the more aware we become of 'unexpected' consequences that produce regret and sorrow. But the Lord has promised to help us through difficult times. Prayer is highly 'under-rated' and it is only those who actually 'pray' who become aware that the Lord DOES hear and answer prayers in unusual ways. One of my prayers actually delivered a real 'tapestry' weaving. The Lord blessed my life with Kelly, who became a friend who stayed in my home with her son for a year as I worked 'night and day' to acquire funds to finish an apartment on the lower level of my home for my father. When she left, she gave me a beautiful tapestry weaving. The image on the tapestry contains a man standing on a bucket playing a fiddle, with a man and woman holding hands, looking deeply into one another's eyes. Their feet actually leave the ground in tune to the music. The Lord used this tapestry to reveal to me that when we keep our eyes on HIM and LISTEN for his still small voice, His Holy Spirit will empower us to feel as though we are 'flying' through our day in harmony with Him even through life's interruptions, and challenges. We are encouraged when we experience the power of the Lord actually working 'through us' and providing answers our prayers.

As I prayed about this book, and what I would include for introductions to each chapter, the Lord arranged for me to leave my home to mail a package at the very same time that my friend, Kelly was at the Post Office. I had not seen her for years. When I saw her, she said, "Hi, do you know who I am?" I replied, "Absolutely Kelly, I am so grateful to you! And I remember the day when I met you and you and your Mom walked up the road to discuss your help with my home. You came at a time when you had a need, and I had a need. You left me with a gift of the tapestry that I still treasure." This is a perfect example of how the Lord is able to connect us with His perfect timing in answer to prayer.

THE FEBRUARY LETTERS

February 7, 2020   Hi (name),

It is snowing so hard today that we can hardly see more than 200 feet. When I got up there was a layer of 2 inches of snow and ice and that was covered with another 3 inches of fluffy snow already on the ground. We now have another 5 inches. Fabien is out plowing already to stay ahead of it. The Weather channel forecast 1-2 feet, and if it doesn't let up, they could be right! What is most wonderful is that none of us here have to drive in it! All of us work from home. My trip to Burlington on Weds on I-89 had 3 cars off the road just after the St. Albans on ramp. What was amazing is that I came through right after it happened. None of the vehicles were damaged, they all hit ice, and two made 180 turns and ended up facing 'north' instead of south in the ditch on the left. I was concerned about the rest of the trip and thought perhaps I should cancel my appointments, but by the time I got to the next Georgia exit, I drove right out of that storm! The Sun was out and the roads had no snow whatsoever. Vermont has weather lines of 'demarcation' between Highgate, Burlington and Shelburne. Sometimes I will call my sister in Georgia, and she is getting lots of snow, and we are getting nothing in Highgate, or visa-versa. A few weeks ago, there was no snow anywhere but I had to go to Shelburne, and right after the 89 Exit, Route 7 was covered with about 6 inches of heavy wet snow! Nothing in Burlington at all!

Northside is presenting the book of Nehemiah. This book covers 11 years full of twists, turns and unexpected events. Not very different than our lives. Nehemiah's problem needs to be solved, and Nehemiah begins to pray about it, and then waits for an answer. The 'waiting' is the hardest of all to do. There are always desired outcomes. Waiting is hard when nothing seems to be happening. When the pastor asked for word to described how it feels to wait, people yelled out, "FRUSTRATING" and there were many voices saying "HARD!" The Pastor added that there is actually a purpose for us during our waiting. "Waiting" is not 'wasted time'. We, too, can go to the Lord and pray, and exercise faith in the goodness of God who has promised to work all things for good to them that love God, who are called according to His purpose. Truly the Lord can fill our waiting with assurance of His presence even in the trial itself. One of those promises was in my Bible reading yesterday:

"My help cometh from the Lord, which made heaven and earth" (Psalm 121:2) and "The Lord will not cast off forever but though he cause grief yet will he have compassion according to the multitude of His mercies." (Lamentations 3:32).

"To everything there is a season and a time for every purpose under Heaven" (Ecclesiastes 3:1) "I will WAIT upon the Lord that hideth his face from the house of Jacob and I will look for Him: (Isaiah 8:17).

Ironically my whole week of Bible reading has focused on WAITING. Today's verse: "Wait on the Lord, be of good courage and he shall strengthen thy heart. Wait I say. . on the Lord" (Psalm 27:14).

I drew a picture of a small seed of a tree, and then of a shoot, and then of its roots going deeper and the top growing higher. I wrote a note: "Growth takes time." The main purpose of our life is for us to GROW in our knowledge of the Lord, and that requires time. It is 'waiting' that creates opportunities to pray. Look up to Him for His help! For me, knowing that He is with me, even in the midst of the trials of life is one of His greatest treasures of all! It is a priceless 'reward' for all who 'believe' and seek Him daily! So, Lord, provide us with the faith we need to 'believe' and to be willing to 'wait' upon you for your will to be done in and through us. To 'trust' that you **_ARE_** indeed in control!

February 13, 2020 Dear (name),

Fabien is enjoying his 'man cave'. When I opened my garage door, he was sitting in front of his wood stove in his comfy chair, feet crossed, and arms folded. He has a ceiling fan with a light that he is getting ready to put up, that will push the stove heated air back down in the area that he enjoys sitting in. He has his radio playing! He might even be doing a 'jig' out there on the garage floor every once in a while. I have to make sure he doesn't add a couch! One time when I went out to check on him, just as I walked in, the song we played at our wedding was playing. I went and pulled him away from his work shelf, and started to dance with him to 'our song' – he was so surprised he didn't even realize it was 'our song' that was playing but indeed it was! It was a special moment for both of us for sure! Last year, he added door with a window and that provides light. That light makes the space feel more spacious. He has his projects going, and can decide which ones he wants to work on and when. What a life!?

Chad has his woods tapped and is getting ready for the first sap run, which could happen this week. His brother Chris is going to be around to help. Fabien worked last week most of the week clearing the roads through the woods with his chainsaw of the fallen trees so that others could travel with their 4 wheelers and work to get the branches and downed trees off the lines that are 'here and there'.

The snow gage stick on our back deck shows 17" of snow. We got more snow today, and more is coming before Sunday. Dean is using snowshoes to tap his woods. The snow in Waterville is so deep there that is the best way to get around. Fabien told me it is slow to use them. There is a lot of hard work that goes into harvesting the sweet crop of maple syrup each year.

Sunday's message was about how success only happens when we follow the ground rules that God has put in place. That requires us to just get along, and work together assessing problems, and enlisting others to help us. Each of us has the challenge of developing habits that help us to make appropriate use of our time and talents. Whatever goal we have, requires work, and an ability to stick with things until they are done, i.e., don't give up! don't quit! And what is pleasing to God is when we give thanks to Him each day, no matter how hard the day! The wonderful thing is that God has asked us to only live 'today'. And he has divided that into 'moments'. When we focus on just the moment at hand, the Lord is able to give us the energy to do what is required for that 'very moment'. When I am in a moment it can seem like time 'stands still' and I am surprised that the day has passed so quickly- because time has seemed to 'stopped entirely'.

This week I told the Lord I wanted to do something special for Fabien for Valentine's day. Something different and special. Well, the Lord has a sense of humor for sure. I boiled eggs to make deviled eggs and one of them when I cut it in half contained a perfect heart shaped yoke, even the yoke itself had formed into a heart shape. Don't ask me how!? So, on February 13 for dinner, I gave Fabien his dinner with that egg sliced on the plate. I told him Happy early Valentine's Day! He said, "Must have been a happy chicken to give such a 'lovely egg'!" This falls into the category of "with God all things are possible" Matthew 19:26).

God's 'currency' comes in the smallest of things and creates special moments for us of unique 'joy' in the midst of our very chaotic and challenging world. "Currency' that is indeed 'priceless'. Lord, open our 'eyes' to see your wondrous ways!

May the Lord bless and keep you and make His face to shine upon you - as you Look up to Him for His help!

February 21, 2020   Dear (name),

I got to babysit my sister Treya's Yorkie today, Cricket. She is recovering from pulling a muscle in her back right leg, so she is struggling to walk and must be carried around in her bed. When Treya leaves her with us, she goes on a food strike. Today, when I gave her the dog food that she just loves – she refused to eat it. Well, no harm there, our new 'not so little kitten' Grady was happy to eat that right up! Audrey told me, 'Grady is an easy cat to have, because he will eat anything, and he is growing fast!" And Grady can move! He uses chairs, tables, and window sills like his own private obstacle course. Itt seems he is trying to outdo his own speed as he jumps from one thing to another, and another. Then he just crashes to sleep and then gets up and do it all over again! He is too young to be 'fixed' but that will surely slow him down!

Fabien's ceiling fan is now installed. It was work for him to figure it out because there weren't instructions with it. He planned to install it at his farmhouse in a bedroom above a bed, but that never happened. Now he will us it in his work area. We are now thinking about Spring and our garden. Today we went and picked up a motorized tiller for our garden rows to help us with the weeding this year. They are expensive new, but a family was moving from VT to FL and sold us the one they had put in storage. I told Fabien I hoped he could get it to run. He replied, "Well, 'you win some and you lose some', and we will win if it works because we got it for a good price."

My brother needed new zippers put in his insulated pants, so I installed new zippers. Most zipper installations require the zipper itself be sewn down, and sewing machine needles can break when they hit the 'teeth' of a zipper. I prayed that the Lord would help me and I managed not to break a needle! Hopefully, both of these new zippers will hold. One was for a pant leg bottom, a very smart idea for putting on boots!

Now we have 15" of snow on our deck. I know soon there will be 'none'. Time passes so quickly.

I just was told about a man who was born without arms and legs: Nick Vijicic. He has become a national inspirational speaker who says 'Finish well' no matter what life has dealt you. We are instructed by the Lord to exercise FAITH, to BELIEVE and to WAIT and hold onto the mystery of Faith (which is NOT according to our own understanding) with a pure conscience.

It is our 'heart' that the Lord treasures. "Spiritual riches enable us to bear temporal losses with great patience." says Charles Spurgeon. There is great peace in knowing that the Lord **HEARS** our prayers and that He will answer them for His name's sake, in His own time and in His own way. When our heart desires fellowship with God, we have access to peace from 'His presence alone' as we go through our day. Then, it matters not where we are, or what we are doing, because in that very place "He is with us -in that moment – like this 'moment'. Jesus said, "Lo I am with you, even to the end of the world" (Matthew 28:20). Between now and then, we have something in common with Nick. We are pilgrims and foreigners. We are to value what is 'not seen' more than 'what is seen'. We must not quit having FAITH in a God who can work the bad for our good – rather we must RUN to Him! Jesus Christ did just that! He cried out to God, and God answered by raising Him from the GRAVE. Jesus now gives eternal life to 'whosever' calls upon His name and in FAITH believes, and accepts His forgiveness, restoration and redemption thru His work for us on that cross. Praise His Holy Name! Jesus enables us to move forward 'in spite of ourselves – in spite of what 'we' think!"

February 28, 2020   Dear (name),

This week is school vacation. We had two young boys over to our home to pound nails with hammers into wood. Fabien set them up with a wooden stump and a tray of nails and handed each of them a hammer. He then showed them how to use the weight of the hammer to help with getting the nails into the wood. They both put in a lot of nails. Then they got blocks of wood with marks for nails for their initials and then used tape to wrap around the nails so their names appeared. Then, they both used Fabien's binoculars and also got to blow his whistle as loud as they could outside. They enjoyed playing with Grady, too. Grady is now taking my sister's socks and has decided to store them under beds, bureaus, chairs. Audrey realized she was running out of socks but she had no idea where they were going. She was smart enough to ask those boys to find the cat toys and they found not only the toys, but all of her missing socks!

Mystery solved!

Audrey's chickens stopped laying eggs because they are unable to take their dust baths. Audrey got play sand and I added it to the chicken coop. It was still too cold at first but the next day it warmed up and they got into it to clean off mites and 'bathe'. We, too, all feel better when we are able to 'clean up'. I saw a parallel with my own heart, when I am 'cold' towards the Lord, I am not very interested in anything to do with the Lord, and that hinders me from the fruit of His righteousness (love, joy, peace longsuffering, gentleness, goodness, faith, meekness, temperance) in my life. The work is to get 'plugged in' by reading the Bible. When we are 'down' is EXACTLY the time that we need to 'THANK God for WHO HE IS and for WHAT HE IS DOING in our lives: this stretches our faith, prunes us by circumstances, and that enables us to bear more fruit. It is Ironic that it is just **when we are at our lowest**, that we are placed *where we are able to give Him all the glory and praise* for what He does. This is because we know it is a 'result' of His intervention in answer to our prayer, and not from anything that 'we' ourselves have done! Like the song, "Vessels only Blessed Master working through us, thou canst use us, every day and every hour."

Fabien's tiller is fixed- - it just needed a new filter, so he is very excited! So am I, because it means we have a way to 'weed' the rows in the garden without having to pull them up all the time!

Fabien has continued to help his son Chad with getting his new sugar house working. The fuel line got hooked up outside and the crew was there to get things running properly. Fabien showed up just as they were experiencing a problem with pulling the fuel with a vacuum to get the fuel to flow into the evaporator rig. Fabien suggested that they fill the line from inside by pumping the fuel into the line from the inside of the sugar house out, rather than keep attempting to get it to flow 'in' from 'outside'. They tried that and hat worked perfectly. Once they filled the pipe from the inside, they were able to get fuel to the evaporator rig and it fired right up! What is amazing is the 'timing' of Fabien's arrival and the fact that he had the answer for them on how to make it work after they had been struggling with the problem for quite a while. The fuel had to go up about 10 feet and then back down into the sugarhouse.

Today I pondered the reality of Jesus's promise of life 'forever' in a perfect place. Just stop and think about this! The very thought of It lessens the weight of burdens, and makes trials less overwhelming. Charles Spurgeon wrote: "We are like 'roses' cut and cast into the 'still for creating perfume" which is 'pleasing' to God." When we pick up our cross and 'push through' we follow Jesus's example of 'setting his face like a flint' to go to Jerusalem where he would be obedient to death on the cross - a 'sacrifice' so well pleasing' to God – that God raised Him from the grave. This paved the way for all who trust in His work to have this forever eternal life in a perfect place called heaven. What a God we serve! How much He loves 'you' and 'me' to do what He did! My heart shouts within me, "Thank you Jesus!"

Chapter 3
The Bridge Builder: The March Letters

Confess your faults one to another and pray for one another that ye may be healed.

James 5:16

One of the biggest challenges in life is to be able to tell someone we are sorry for something we've done. When we 'hurt' someone, we distance ourselves from that person emotionally, and that creates a 'gap' in our relationship with that person. To heal we must become 'bridge builders' and restore our ability to communicate and connect with the person we hurt. Fabien, my husband, has been building a small bridge across a creek. This has taken a lot of work and effort on his part. He cut down dead trees to get the logs needed for a foundation that would be placed horizontally in one direction, and then placed other logs within the 'gaps'. Then he placed logs vertically to create a flat surface to cross over to the other side with his tractor. He in effect created a new walking path through the wooded area.

It is work to undo the wrongs that we have done. A simple "I'm sorry" is like trying to place just one small limb across the creek, with the hope that we will then be able to easily cross over. Gary Chapmam and Joyce Thomas have a book entitled "When Sorry Isn't Enough". His books says that when we are hurt, or when we have been wronged, we do not want to hear, "I'm sorry, BUT!" Chapman and Thomas explain that word 'but' negates our sorry message. My friend Adam said, "That word 'butt' is a very messy word!" We laughed but there is a lot of truth to his statement. No one wants to feel as though 'they' are the reason for a problem occurring. Chapman and Thomas explain the adding of 'but' makes the apology more like an 'excuse' to justify what happened. A true apology needs to include the reason that we are 'sorry. For example, "I am truly sorry that I did not call to let you know I was running late". This lets the person know we understand exactly what has created the issue. To truly heal, we also should include a question, "What can I do to make this up to you?" and a statement that confirms we do not indeed want to do the same thing again, such as, "I am working hard to not do that again". When all of these components are present, true healing will occur. None of us is perfect. We are asked by the Lord to Love Him and then to love one another. When we truly 'repent' a door will open for us to take responsibility for the consequences of our actions. We should also ask the person, "Can you forgive me?" This confirms that we really understand we have created the problem and in effect creates that bridge that allows true forgiveness to cross over to us.

Paul in the Bible states: 'with all lowliness and meekness, with longsuffering, forbearing one another in love, endeavor to keep the unity of the Spirit in the bond of peace" (Ephesians 4:2-3).

THE MARCH LETTERS

March 5, 2020 Dear (name),

We are now down to 7" of snow on our back deck. Fabien's son, Dean, tells us that in Waterville there is still 2 feet of snow in the woods, and he is working to finish tapping his sugar bush with snowshoes which is slow going but better than attempting to walk through deep snow. Yesterday morning there was a cloud that was over the manmade lake here making it impossible to see anything except the trunks of the larger trees. This looked very surreal. I am so grateful that Fabien added another 'come along strap' to brace up our boat dock to prevent the ice breakup from taking the dock down which would then require major repair again this Spring.

This week, Fabien and I were travelling home and a car pulled out in front of his truck. He hit the brakes to prevent hitting the car, and almost succeeded, but the female driver hit the brakes too, and that slowed her car down and we ended up hitting the side back of her car. Both vehicles have damage. His truck headlight, fender, and side fender will need to be repaired. The accident happened on Route 78 just outside of Swanton. Both of us were relieved that it wasn't worse, but it is always a challenge when things like this happen. Her insurance should cover all of his damages, as the accident was due to her not stopping at a stop sign and just driving in front of our truck. No one was hurt, but that car had to be towed. We had a lot of rescue vehicles show up in addition to the State Police. I went around and talked with as many of them as I could and gave them my mini black bears, lions and eagles with Bible books and thanked them for what they do. The State Police asked me to go and speak to the driver of the other vehicle which was a young girl about 16 years old. Fabien had been down to make sure everyone was okay right after impact. when I had made the 911 call. She was visibly shaken, but I was able to give her a little sheep and Bible book. I told her we were fortunate it was not worse, and that the accident would make her and us better drivers in the future. It will take some time for her to feel comfortable driving again. There were a lot of car and truck parts that were in the road from the impact. Emergency people used brooms to sweep the road clear. Fabien and I were both asked to sign a waiver to agree that we did not need a trip to the hospital in their ambulance. Fabien was amazingly calm during and after impact. Me, not so much. I had been sleeping in the passenger side and knew when Fabien hit those brakes hard, that something was really wrong. When I opened my eyes, I saw the impact occur. My seatbelt kept me in my seat, but things in the truck went flying forward to the floor and dash of the truck. Fortunately, Fabien was travelling about 30 mph. When we got home, he went and used his chainsaw in the woods to de-stress. I did my Journal work and that helped me to de-stress and focus on something else. Both of us were reminded of how quickly things can change, and how important it is to appreciate every day and to love one another. "The Lord is a strong hold in the day of trouble and he knoweth them that trust in Him" (Nahum 1:7).

My bible reading today was about God's Pattern for our lives. We are much like Mary and Joseph and Elizabeth and Zacharias. The things that happen in our lives rarely make sense, and are beyond human understanding. We need to yield as they did and say as Mary did, 'Be it done unto me according to thy word'. Our attitude of yieldedness opens doors to be available to God's Holy Spirit. The challenge is to overcome earthly sorrows, disappointments and trials. We, too, ponder the meaning of it all within our hearts. It is an exercise of FAITH in God to be able to say. "Thy will be done, on earth as it is in heaven" God can help us to forgive as we have been forgiven. He can lead us NOT into temptation (disbelieve) and He can deliver us from 'evil'. God's peace comes when we KNOW in our heart that God's Kingdom will come when Jesus returns to the earth to the Mount of Olives from heaven . It is great to know that evil has an end, and His Kingdom of love and peace lasts forever.

March 13, 2020   Dear (name)

Our now juvenile Grady cat has made his first adventure 'outside' – Audrey has worked very hard to pick him up to make sure he does not escape when the outside door is opened, but this morning, he managed to 'run very fast' through her legs, and before she could catch him, out the door he went! Audrey called and asked me to go capture him. But by the time I got outside where he was, Grady had realized he was way too cold, so when Audrey opened the outside door to talk to me, his little legs could not get him back into the house quick enough! We all enjoy Grady! I have been picking him up for 'walk-a-bouts' upstairs, and this week he got to watch the chickens from my bedroom window that were let out of their chicken coup. He placed his paws on my bedroom window and turned his head this way and that way, following them with his head. As I watched him watch those chickens, I felt like the Lord was showing me that when I am reading the Bible, he is able to 'shew me' spiritual things, too, from on 'high' that I could see no other way, and my heart rejoiced to know how much the Lord loves it when we desire to be close to Him, rewarding us 'in kind'.

The estimate for the truck has come in. Seems it does not take much these days to rack up a bill. We are at $4500, and very thankful that insurance will cover the total cost for repair.

Fabien's son, Chad, has made ¼ of his crop of syrup so far, and this week should have great sap runs due to the freezing temps at night and warmer weather during the day. Fabien's son, Dean in Waterville, has 35,000 taps, Chad has 7,000 taps. It felt great to be outside this week without having to have a coat on! The 'time change' is causing a challenge for all of us here. We cannot seem to get onto the new time and are ending up getting up much later than we normally would, but having it light out at night past 7 pm is GREAT! The rain this week has caused all of the snow on our deck to disappear, and most of the snow on our lawn is also gone except for the plowed piles of snow. There is a lot of Spring cleanup to be done as well, but we are all ready to be enjoying 'sitting outside' and having a fire in our fire pit area.

The Northside message continues to follow the account of Nehemiah and the things that came up that were designed to get him to 'stop' building and restoring those walls, just stop him from doing what he was doing. Many were profiting from having the walls not rebuilt, and were determined to keep things the way they were, and worked to get Nehemiah to 'stop'. They started with just asking him to 'come down' to 'talk'. They sent this same message to Nehemiah not just once but 4 times, and 4 times he said 'no'. There is quite a message there for all of us who choose to walk by faith! The persistent forces of evil will work hard to get us off 'task' with their goal of diverting us from the main purpose of our service to the Lord, too!

"Some trust in chariots, and some in horses, but we will remember the name of the Lord our God" (Psalm 20:7).

"We will rejoice in thy salvation, and in the name of our God we will set up our banners: The Lord fulfil all thy petitions" (Psalm 20:5).

I have a 'note' written in my Bible on Psalm 23 – that this Psalm is for the PRESENT and that the Lord will: Restore, Lead, Comfort, and Prepare a 'table' for us in the presence of our enemies. What is of great comfort is that the Shepherd of our soul does not abandon us – we are His sheep, and each day, His Holy Spirit surrounds and sends angels to help and protect us. Praise His Holy Name! "The earth is the Lord's and the fulness thereof, the world and they that dwell therein" (Psalm 24.1).

We are to "cast your care upon Him, and seek His face, for He careth for 'you'!" (1 Peter 5:7).

March 19, 2020 Dear (name),

If you are not getting the news, the world is pretty much shut down due to the corona virus in an attempt to prevent spreading of the COVID19 virus, and to get things back to normal as soon as possible. My family feels very blessed to be located where we are, and to have the benefit of not having to travel. I am very grateful to work from home. The University of Vermont is shut down along with all of the schools now, as well as restaurants, and even going to church cannot be done because it is a gathering of more than 25. I absolutely LOVE being home, so this is not any sacrifice for me. My prayer is that the Lord will provide a way of escape for our world and that He will help us to care for one another as we can.

We have not begun our Spring yard cleanup, still not quite warm enough to be doing that, but this Friday it may be warm enough to do some of it. We are keeping those that are working to get maple syrup and harvesting the trees of sap in our prayers for a good crop this year. The ice is now off our manmade lake and the view of seeing the water again is quite wonderful! Ice does not reflect the trees or shoreline. I truly enjoy having that special view from my office desk area as I work on my Journals.

And here is something to make you smile. We got together to have sugar on snow today with everyone. Brought back some childhood memories for sure!

With the snow disappearing, Fabien has been taking me and others on his deer watching expeditions. We ride in his truck on the roads up here with binoculars looking for turkeys and deer. We have now been twice and have seen about 50 deer and 50 turkeys each time. He says they are hungry, but they look very healthy as well. Having the ground uncovered allows them to be out foraging for corn, and grains. Fabien's cousin, Lester, came to spend the night this past weekend and we enjoyed venison steak and venison sausage with eggs for breakfast, delicious.

Fabien has been working on the canoe port path and has created a beautiful bench made from 2 tree stumps and a tree trunk cut in half. It is quite a delight to go on the path now and have a place to sit down! He will set a few other of these 'tree benches' up along the walkway. He has been given permission to harvest the wood from the area, and our wood pile is now quite high. Last fall, we gave most of our stored wood to his son who was in need, and it seems the Lord has provided with likely triple what we gave away. The promise that we cannot 'out give' the Lord.

"Give, and it shall be given unto you; good measure, pressed down, and shaken together, and running over, shall men give into your bosom. For with the same measure that ye mete withal it shall be measured to you again" (Luke 6:38).

March 27, 2020   Dear (name),

This week we had what is called 'sugar snow' and one more magnificent view of snow-covered trees with bright white carpets of snow covering everything. We had enough to shovel and I actually stopped to make some snow angels, which was not so successful in seeing my 'angel wings' on the ground, but they delivered inner joy knowing the Lord has angels assigned to watch over us. Within a few hours all of it 'evaporated' as though it had been a mirage. A reminder to me of how quickly things can change and that today's issues will also 'disappear' in His time! The Lord **IS** able to answer our prayers – but we do have a part. What is our part?

". . . and if I send pestilence among my people; If my people, which are called by my name, shall humble themselves, and pray, and seek my face, and turn from their wicked ways; then will I hear from heaven, and will forgive their sin, and will heal their land" (2 Chronicles 7:13-14).

May the Lord help us to pray, listen and follow His Holy Spirit's leading. We must be willing to repent of choosing happiness apart from His holiness, and of seeking 'rest apart from His presence' – for neither deliver what we seek. Without Him, we find only temporary pleasures with no lasting happiness -happiness only comes as a RESULT of having fellowship with Him. Seeking 'rest' through earthly 'distractions' creates anxiety and results in fear.

When we pray about everything, we will find that we will not be worried about anything! When we are 'afraid' we need to RUN like a little chick to God and go under His wings of his eternal Love. Quick real prayers: 'Help me, help me, help me!" or "Lord, deliver and protect me and my family for your name's sake!' Work!

Here is my version of Psalm 91 turned into a prayer:

Lord let me dwell in the secret place of the most High – let me abide under the shadow of the Almighty. Be thou my refuge and my fortress: for you ARE my God; and in YOU I trust.

Deliver me Lord from the snare of the fear of the unknown; make a way for our world, especially America, to escape the snare of this pestilence. Cover us Lord like a bird would its chicks with your feathers, with the protection found under Your wings, Help me Lord to trust in your truth THAT 'you are God and that YOU ARE in CONTROL of ALL THINGS and that you are working these 'things' for our good --let this knowledge become a shield and buckler for emotions – help us to walk by FAITH in what is NOT seen, and enable us to not be afraid for the terror by night that comes from the nightly news; nor for the arrow that flyeth by day that shoots at us from inner fears. Lord keep us from harm - let us to not walk in the dark and to not be afraid of being destroyed at noonday.

I ask these things in your precious Holy Name for YOUR glory and for YOUR honor! THANK YOU AND PRAISE YOU LORD, for hearing our prayers. Help us Lord to patiently wait and to continue to go to you in heaven with our concerns and ask you in prayer for help every day!

Chapter 4

Above the Maze: The April Letters

Set your affection on things above, not on things on the earth.

Colossians 3:2

There is a 60-acre corn maze in Dixon, California, that causes people to get lost and actually have to be rescued from the field. People head into the maze with confidence, map in hand, believing they can quickly navigate themselves to the end without any problem. Afterall, they have a map! However, once 'inside' the maze field, it suddenly becomes quite easy to lose track of where you are located. Most, take out their cell phone and end up calling 911. The call dispatches a helicopter to their location, and then they are told how to get out.

We also enter life full of excitement and expectations but also find ourselves in situations where we, too, need to ask someone to help us. Each of us likely will find ourselves in situations in which asking for help will be critical to survive mentally, and emotionally.

Each life contains its very own 'maze field' but we have assurance that we can get above the problems when we are willing to go 'vertical' in prayer to the Lord. Many troubles in life have no easy answer, and no easy solution. And, we are likely to be asked to bear more than we ever expected we would have to deal with. Just as 911 rescuers show up to help, believers are asked to 'show up' to help those we love. We are told to remember that everything in this life is 'temporary'. Job cried out, "Naked I came out of my mother's womb, and naked shall I return thither, the Lord gave, the Lord hath taken away, blessed be the name of the Lord" (Job 1:21). Timothy exclaims, "For we brought nothing into this world, and it is certain we shall carry nothing out" (1 Timothy 6:7).

April 2, 2020 Dear (name)

Easter is Sunday April 12. Most people know about the miracles of Jesus, and of his crucifixion. Few know all the details of Good Friday and after. The guards parted his garments and cast lots for them. Jesus refused a drink and utters, "Father forgive them for they know not what they do". He is mocked by the Jews, 'He saved others, himself, he cannot save." The thieves talk, one says, "Remember me when thou comest into thy Kingdom" and hears Jesus say, 'Today thou shalt be with me in paradise." Jesus says "Woman behold thy son" and then looks at John. Darkness at Noon, and Jesus cries, "My God, my God, why hast thou forsaken me!". 'I thirst," "It is finished!" "Into thy hands I commend my spirit!" Then a great earthquake, and the veil in the Jewish temple is tore in two. Graves are opened and many from those graves appear to those alive. The centurion said, "Truly this was the Son of God." Joseph of Arimathea begged the body of Jesus and Pilate agreed. Jesus was placed in Joseph's tomb and a great stone was rolled over the door. The chief priests asked that Pilate put a guard on the tomb and he set a watch. On the first day of the week Mary Magdalene and the other Mary went with spices to the sepulcher, and behold there was a great earthquake and the angel of the Lord descended from heaven, and came and rolled back the stone from the door and sat upon it. The keepers did shake, and became as dead men. And the angel answered and said unto the women, "Fear not ye, for I know that ye seek Jesus which was crucified, He is not here for he is risen as he said, Come see the place where the Lord lay." They went and told the disciples and Peter and John ran to the tomb and they saw the linen cloths lying and Peter went into the sepulcher and seeth the linen cloths lie, and the napkin that was about his head not lying with the linen clothes, but wrapped together in a place by itself. But Mary Magdalene stood without at the sepulcher weeping and stooped down and looked into the sepulcher and seeth two angels, one at the head, and the other at the feet where the body of Jesus had lain. They say unto her, "Woman, why weepest thou?" She saith unto them," Because they have taken away my Lord, and I know not where they have laid him" and when she had thus said, she turned herself back, and saw Jesus but supposing him to be the gardener, saith unto him, "Sir if thou have borne him hence, tell me where thou hast laid him, and I will take him away." Jesus saith unto her, "Mary." She saith unto him, "Rabbani, which is to say, Master." Jesus saith unto her, "Touch me not for I am not yet ascended to my Father, but go to my brethren and say unto them, "I ascent unto my Father, and your Father and to my God and your God." Mary Magdalene came and told the disciples that she had seen the Lord, and that he had spoken these things unto her. That evening when the disciples were assembled for fear of the Jews came Jesus and stood in the midst and saith unto them, "Peace be unto you." But Thomas was not with them. When told, he did not believe and said, "Except I shall see in his hands the print of the nails, and put my finger into the print of the nails, and thrust my hand into his side, I will not believe." Eight days later, Thomas was with them and Jesus appeared and said, "Peace be unto you" and said to Thomas, "Reach hither thy finger and behold my hands, and reach hither thy hand and thrust it into my side, and be not faithless but believing, and Thomas answered and said, "My Lord and my God." Jesus saith unto him, "Thomas because thou hast seen me, thou hast believed, blessed are they that have not seen, and yet have believed." And Jesus appeared many times for 40 days. Then he went to the Mount of Olives and gave the great commission to: 'Go, and tell all nations the good news." Then he went up and a cloud received him out of their sight. And while they looked steadfastly toward heaven as he went up, behold two men stood by them in white apparel which also said, "Ye men of Galilee why stand ye gazing up into heaven? This same Jesus which is taken up from you into heaven, shall so come in like manner as ye have seen him go into Heaven." So, 'look up' Jesus will return in the air for His own" (2 Thes 5: 14-17) (1 Cor 15: 51-57).

April 9, 2020 Dear (name)

We had the largest full moon of 2020 last night. We have continued to have frost at night so the sap is still running but things are being shut down now. Fabien's son, Chad, says he will finish up today.
Fabien and I worked to set up our tree swing using his tractor bucket. His tractor makes the job a lot easier than with a ladder. We have it on a large maple tree which has some compromised limbs higher up and will need to be taken down. We are giving this tree one more summer for us to enjoy it!

Grady has managed to jump through Audrey's chair barrier in front of her door and has gotten outside again. Fabien was right there and able to rescue him from a 'cat fight' with our neighbor's calico cat who immediately challenged Grady. Fabien grabbed him as he hunched his back up to the fight! Once again, not a scratch on him! And he has another great lesson under his belt so to speak.

Still too cold for us to have a fire in our fire pit. Fabien planted blueberry plants that were given to us by my sister, Dayle, from our farm. I planted strawberry plants that she also gave us. Our back deck is cleaned off and we now have 2 places to sit outside. This time of year, is busy but contains a lot of 'waiting'.

'Waiting' is one of those attributes that requires us to mix 'patience' with 'faith". This is the only way for us to have a sense of real 'peace' during trouble. Almost everyone is taking precautions to prevent contracting the corona virus! Our complex lives have become more challenging. Right now, any "Normalcy" feels priceless. THIS life IS 'temporary' which makes personal ASSURANCE of heaven a TOP priority for each of us. Jesus said, "Whosoever believeth in me, shall never die." Jesus Christ (the 2nd Adam/who was created perfect and remained perfect through perfect choices) over 2000 years ago died on a cross and God resurrected Him. Jesus was seen for over 40 days alive by over 500 people prior to His ascension into heaven (Acts 15:6). Salvation is a RESULT of our uttering similar words as the thief on the cross, "Remember me when I come into your Kingdom". Jesus's reply to that thief was:, "Today thou shalt be with me in paradise!" This requires only our verbal FAITH – which is very much like an "I do" of FAITH in God, and secures an eternal marriage covenant that we get to make with Him while we are on earth. God seeks to abide with us. God can help us to love ourselves, and one another. Those who 'call upon His name' gain His Holy Spirit within who is able to 'add' to FAITH, virtue and to virtue patience, and to patience, godliness and to godliness brotherly kindness and to brotherly kindness charity" (1 Peter 1:5-7).

From Heaven's perspective, troubles are a 'blessing' because they cause 'change'. They open Spiritual doors to God's love and peace. And HIS love will work through us, to the degree we yield our life and time to Him. "Sadly, we can live 'in' God yet _choose_ to remain many degrees distant from Him." (Charles Spurgeon)

Soooo . . *let patience have her perfect work. (James 1:4-8).* And...

Look up -- pestilence is one of the end times indicators for the Lord's return in the air for His own.

April 18, 2020 (name)

Fabien's son, Chad is over 80 barrels- hoping to make his goal of 90. My week is changed as one of my sister's was diagnosed with pneumonia and has to be on drugs and I am going to work to help her out.

Am reading Phillip Keller's book entitled "Rabbani – which is to say Master" which covers the entire Bible from Genesis to Revelation. This book contains the scriptures in the Old Testament that relate to Jesus Christ being foretold as coming, and the rituals of Jewish Temple ceremonies with the 'sacrificial lambs'. One of his statements was 'riveting': that the opposite of 'love' is not 'hate' but rather 'just not caring'. The reason this jumped out at me is because my life is very full. It does require my to exercise a great deal of discipline to take 'action' – consistently. Caring for His sheep takes time and energy. This simple observation reveals so very much as to the 'why' our current world is in the 'state' it is in. We are bombarded daily with 'information' that is 'empty' and 'useless' to us for the main purpose of our being here which is to 'care' for one another. My prayer is that we will read the Bible, for those words do link us to 'HIS Spirit' and empower our 'heart' – to actually care, and His "Holy Spirit" provides us the energy to care for each another.

This week is the week of Jesus's death, burial and resurrection. Fabien and I watched a feature on Billy Graham that featured an interview with Franklin Graham. He explained how his Father, Billy, had visited a prison that made 'caskets' Billy ordered 2 of them – one for his Mom and one for his Dad. The caskets were simple pine boxes made from plywood with a wooden cross on the top. The video clips showed the man who made the caskets and the very casket that was used for Billy's funeral service at the White House in the Rotunda. Franklin shared that his Dad was thrilled to know he was going home and most amazingly had told everyone he would make it to 100 years old. Franklin explained that when they added the 9 months (from his conception as a baby) to his age- he died at exactly 100 years old. Billy Graham's message of salvation is for each of 'us' individually and depends upon each of us calling upon the Lord. There is NOTHING we can do to MERIT salvation, but rather Jesus came so that each of us would have the opportunity to cry out to Him – as the thief on the cross did – and ask for forgiveness and to be remembered when we come into His kingdom.

I personally listen for a 'trumpet' sound and for the voice of the archangel, and am 'looking up'.

"Praise and Thank you, Jesus, for Your amazing love for us – for coming to earth, and living as a 'man', and for living in obedience to the leading of God's Holy Spirit. Help us, Lord, to encourage one another to not be overwhelmed with 'evil' but to overcome 'evil' with good."

Keeping you ever in our prayers. "Behold: The Lamb of God" (John 1:35).

April 23, 2020 Dear (name)

Grady had his nails trimmed. The task required my sister, Treya, to hold him as my sister, Audrey, worked to carefully cut his nails. His favorite toy is a mouse on a stick that squeaks. He has a 'cat tunnel maze' with three exits that he runs through. Audrey says he will be a very large cat because of the size of his paws and the length of his tail. When I pick him up for a 'walk about' he has his favorite windows in different rooms that he likes to be carried to look out of! Audrey continues to have socks missing and he continues to hide them under bureaus, and beds and tables.

We got horse manure for the garden this year. Fabien wanted to try it as he has a friend that used it and felt it worked better than cow manure. Sunday, we started seeds inside with a grow light and the cabbage, broccoli and spinach are all up. Fabien picked up another cattle watering trough from his farm to use as a raised bed in our garden. Both of us are looking forward to being able to stand up to harvest the plants placed in these containers.

Fabien has his wood pile all split. The wood still needs to be stacked but the area looks much better and the path is open again.

Our neighbor friends, Caroline and Adam, called for some 'advice'.' Their washing machine hose detached from the wall and sprayed water all over their carpeted floor. Fabien and I went to help. He was able to cut out the base of the cabinet to pull out the wet carpet. It was quite a job. His knees hurt and the space was tight to work in, but he got it done! Once we were home, he joked, "Well that was really a LOT more than advice!"

Another of our neighbors will move this week. Fabien and I went Tuesday for 7 am to help them to load a trailer with their belongings.

Polly and Bobby, our friends, will return to VT from May 1. They have a camper and will stay at camp grounds here and there – some are open. Still cold here. We had snow this am and it was 22 degrees but good for Fabien's son, Dean, who is still boiling for maple syrup.

The COVID19 virus has made me want to connect with old friends. I have taken time to either call or write and it has been great to re-connect. I send out a text Bible verse daily. Today's verse: "These things have I spoken unto you that **IN ME** ye might have peace, In the world ye SHALL HAVE tribulation, **but be of good cheer** *I have overcome the world*" (John 16:33).

Dwelling in God is possible by starting and ending each day with Bible time and prayer, praying throughout the day for His help, and thanking Him.

"Inspire me still to do THY will – Grant to me each- that greater wealth of an undefiled and loyal heart - until the race is won, make Thou my pathway plain – TEACH me THY way."

Chapter 5

Bear Ye Another's Burdens – The May Letters

Bear ye one another's burdens, and so fulfill the law of Christ.

Galatians 6:2

God rewards us in special ways when we are willing to be involved in meaningful ways with others. This is what produces the 'abundant' life. The Lord promised in John 10:10 "I come that they might have life, and that they may have it more abundantly."

My friend Tami (who designs the covers for my books) shared with me that her mother, Lynne, was in a rehabilitation facility near where I live. She explained, "My Mom was always very active in her life. She was always doing things. She was very smart; at the head of her class. Now, she's no longer able to walk, and spends her days in bed or in a chair and she rarely talks." I knew Tami's experience first-hand. As I listened, I thought of my own mother who also ended up in a nursing home, and I felt a deep desire to help. I said, "Is it okay if I go and visit her?" My own visits to see my Mom were challenging and having another person go with me, helped a lot. I told Tami I would go with her when she visited her! Tami agreed, "That would be good, feel free to stop and check in on her when you can!"

During my first visit, to see her Mom, there was soft music playing and Lynne was resting with her eyes closed in her bed. I went and stood beside her bed. I placed my hand softly on her arm and introduced myself, "Hi Lynne, I am one of your daughter Tami's best friends, I am so glad to meet you!"

As I spoke, I reached and held her hand. I said, "You need to know that you did a wonderful job raising your family!" I looked around and noticed a family picture on the wall. I said, "There's a picture of Tami right on the wall! You need to know she is an amazing graphic artist. Her projects are truly incredible. Tami is really creative and is highly respected by all."

I then placed my hand gently on the top of her head and stroked her hair and said, "You are LOVED, Lynne, so very much!" Then, I noticed there was a picture of her on another bulletin board. I went and got that picture and took it and held the picture up to her. She now had opened her eyes. She pointed to the picture and said, "That's me!" I replied, "Yes! it is YOU! What any incredible life you have had, Lynne! You and Tami are very much alike!" I read a letter I found on the board to her that she had written, and told her it was a great letter. As I got ready to leave, I said, "I will come and visit you again soon!"

Then, I called Tami to let her know that her Mom had actually spoken to me and had acknowledged her picture. I continued to stop in to see Lynne and brought her scrapbooks that contained pictures of birds, and mountains and flipped through them with her, as she watched me turn the pages. I also brought a bird mobile to go above her bed for her room. My hope was that Tami and I would get an opportunity to visit her Mom together but our different work schedules made that a challenge.

Then, one week, Tami and I arranged to meet for breakfast. After breakfast, we both hugged and left to do our tasks. My first stop was to go and visit her Mom, Lynne. When I arrived at the Rehab Center, I was shocked and excited to see Tami standing in the lobby area! Neither of us had discussed visiting her Mom but here we were! A divine arrangement!

Finally, we got to visit her together. Seeing Tami and her Mom together was a priceless treasure to me from the Lord. God, indeed blesses us when we share our burdens.

When COVID started, all of the hospitals and Elder Care facilities were closed to visitors and no one was allowed inside. There were also restrictions on restaurants, but when these lifted, Tami and I agreed to meet for breakfast again. We had not seen each other for several months. As we sat down, we started to visit, and Tami began to look really sad. I wondered how her Mom was doing. She told me she needed to tell me something but could not find the words. As I watched, she took a napkin and wrote words on it and handed it to me. It read, "My Mom has died." As I read the words, tears came to my eyes.

Tami explained that the facility had called her and allowed her to come and be with her Mom during the last few days of her life. That was a wonderful gift. She had prayed and asked the Lord for time to be with her to hear her talk, and although that had not happened, she was with her when she passed.

My own visits with Lynne had opened a door for me to pray with her. During each of my visits, before I left, I would hold her hand and pray. On one of my last visits, I told her, "Lynne, Jesus has prepared a place for you in heaven. He died to give you eternal life, and whoever calls upon his name will be young again, and will live forever in a perfect place called, heaven." I then took her hand, and told her, "One of the two thieves on the cross asked Jesus to remember him, and Jesus replied to him, 'Today, you will be with me in paradise!' Then, as I held Lynne's hand, I said, "This is a prayer I am saying on your behalf: "Lord, remember me when I come into Your kingdom!" I then assured her, 'These things are written that you may KNOW that you have eternal life (1 John 3:17). When I finished those words, Lynne squeezed my hand.

As I held Tami's note, I said, "Tami, we **WILL** see your Mom again in heaven!"

THE MAY LETTERS

May 1, 2020   Dear (name),

Grady managed to 'escape' to the great outdoors today. Fabien and I were not home to help catch him. Audrey finally gave up and left the porch door open for him. He chased leaves and ran around, but finally came back, cold and tired, and then went to sleep. She told me he was out there for about 1 hr.

Our daffodils are in full bloom. Our fruit trees have buds. Fabien rototilled the garden and sowed buckwheat. He will till this under once it comes up to keep the weeds down. We had a lot of wind yesterday but no limbs came down from trees. That is a big relief for sure. My sister, Lisa, lives in Warner Robins, Georgia and she told me the wind there was bad as well. My friend in North Port, Florida also had high winds and rain. They needed the rain so they did not mind the winds that brought it. It is quite cold out today and the winds are still racing through here making it a challenge to stay outside for any length of time.

My seedling tomatoes, and cabbages are ready to transplant into larger containers. That will keep us busy. Fabien obtained some large wall stones last year, and this week he started making a stone wall between our woods and our lawn. The wall is tiered and rounded and about 200' in length. He has made amazing progress in just 4-5 days. He levels each stone as he goes Each stone weighs about 50 lbs. Good that he can carry them with his tractor bucket to the wall location.

We will get our gazebo cover on soon for our back deck. That creates an outdoor seating area out of the sun and rain, and adds a space for visiting with others, just reading, or for meals. Fabien went through our outdoor shed and organized everything. We gifted 4 outdoor chairs to our friends Caroline and Adam for their new home backyard. Fabien is also giving them his push lawn mower. Fabien used that for his lawnmowing business for areas too hard to get to with his Zero-turn. It is perfect for their small yard.

COVID19 opened doors for me to reach out to those friends of mine that I have not contacted in 20 years. From my handwritten notes and emails, almost all have emailed or called. Sweet to reconnect for sure. Fabien and I plan to attend the next Densmore family gathering in Southern Vermont when they have it again. Old neighbors from Colchester and Milton, are trapped in Florida and will not travel back to VT until the restrictions are lifted. One of my friends ate in her car and slept in her car to avoid dealing with people and hotels in order to return to VT.

The challenge is to have faith in God during COVID19. Believers have assurance of 'eternal life' because of Jesus Christ's and His death and resurrection. Jesus said, "He that **believeth in me, though he** were dead, **yet shall he live**: [26] And **whosoever** liveth and **believeth in me shall** never **die**. (John 11:25) for 'whosoever shall call upon the name of the Lord, shall be saved" (Romans 10:13). Christ has promised, 'to be absent from the body is to be present with the Lord" (2 Corinthians 5:8).

"O death, where is thy sting? O grave, where is thy victory?" (1 Corinthians 15:55). "Neither fear ye their 'fear' nor be afraid" (Isaiah 8:12). "For God is with us" (Isaiah 8:10) "Sanctify the Lord of Hosts Himself and let Him be your fear and let Him be your dread" (Isaiah 8:13). "For I reckon that the sufferings of this present time are not worthy to be compared with the glory which shall be revealed in us" (Romans 8:28). You are always in our prayers.

May 7, 2020   Dear (name),

We got our gazebo cover up and our chairs and outdoor table set up this weekend, and we had another fire in our fire pit area. Fabien is working to complete the wall along the wood line and it continues to look amazing.

We felt a 3.1 earthquake that occurred in Bedford Quebec about 10 am on Wednesday. It rattled the entire house. Somewhat scary but nothing fell off of the walls, and it was over within 10 seconds.

Grady continues to grow and can he run! I had to laugh the other day because we have a spiral staircase and up until that day, I had been able to get up the stairs ahead of him, but this week he now has grown up enough to be able to run up those stairs faster than I can!

Our friends are headed back from Florida to Vermont in their camper and should arrive by this weekend. It will be great to have them back in Vermont for sure. My bible readings today were focused on God's strength coming from our 'waiting'. "Their strength is to sit still" (Isaiah 30:7).

"In returning and rest shall be your strength" (Isaiah 30:15).

"Be still and know that I am God, I will be exalted among the heathen, I will be exalted in the earth" (Psalm 46:10).

"Wait on the Lord, be of good courage, and he shall strengthen thine heart: wait, I say, on the Lord" (Psalm 27:14).

Our Northside message this week was from Nehemiah Chapter 9. After they had rebuilt the walls of the City the people gathered to hear the Words from the Bible. The priest, Ezra, provided instructions to them on how to please God. What was true then, is also true today. In order for us to experience the fullness of His power, we must be willing to do the work and to listen to His message. Oftentimes, we are unaware of our hunger because we are literally starving from knowing those words. God blesses us when we seek Him and take time to read His words in the Bible. Our Holy God is gracious to us, and will bring us to confession and worship and provide us with a true passion and love for Him. This busy world makes it a challenge to set aside time to 'read' the Bible, but by taking time to 'sit still' and read those words, we are given the strength we need for the challenges we face.

When our first thoughts of the day are about God, He is faithful to honor us with His presence and to go with us through the day. My friend starts each day with Psalm 19:14: "Let the words of my mouth, and the meditation of my heart, be acceptable in thy sight, O LORD, my strength, and my redeemer."

And when we also pray, God promises to hear and to answer those prayers:

'At the voice of thy cry, when he shall hear it, he will answer thee" (Isaiah 30:19).

"And thine ears shall hear a word behind thee saying, this is the way walk ye in it when ye turn to the right hand and when ye turn to the left" (Isaiah 30:21).

And amazingly, that is exactly what happens!

May 15, 2020   Dear (name),

Finally going to warm up here. Our seedlings are now pretty big, and ready for transplanting outside, but the concern is a frost, so we are holding off for at least another week here. This is my favorite time of the year because of all of the new life, the trees are just starting to have leaves, and our Hosta plants are pushing themselves out of the ground. I have been watching a lone tulip – the only one – and finally it has a bulb on top that looks like it may open in a few days.

Fabien has not mowed our lawn here yet, but Enosburg is mowing and his son, Chad, has had to mow at the farm. Our soil here is very sandy and Fabien says that is why we have a late start each year with the lawn growth. I do love the color of the first green lawn, it is more of a yellowish green and I pops like eye candy. Once grass is cut, it takes on a dark green color.

The COVID19 is pushing all of us with a sense of fear and foreboding.

Whatever 'go to's' we have used in the past to 'cope', are the 'go to's" for comfort now. Fabien's son, Chris, has fallen back into drinking and has had another trip to the hospital. So once again the family is rallying to help him to make his way navigating life with learning how to do things differently. Fabien has spent a few nights with him at his home in Richford.

We had friends this week come to use kayak and canoe. We paddled up to a tree that is hung up on a sand mound under the lake, Fabien told my friend that he had seen a bald eagle land on it, and that it was a good resting place for birds. Then he added, "And there is a 'bald eagle' right in this boat right now!" My friend looked to see, and he said, "ME!" then, he took off his hat to show a bald head. It was truly entertaining! My friend replied, "Well that's a comment from someone who is very much at home in their own body." We all laughed.   We are truly blessed that the Lord can provide:

Peace in Chaos   - Comfort in Loss - Forgiveness in sorrow --Strength in trials

"He hast enlarged my steps under me so that my feet did not slip" (2 Samuel 22:37). This is exactly what is contained within moments of faith. We are asked to just take the next step. Then the next. Then the next. When we are able to look back, we will see silver linings of having God's divine help. The presence of God's Holy Spirit's presence with us during our trials becomes its own reward. When I walk at night or in the early morning when it is still dark out, I am able to see enough light from the street light to make it to that light. And then from that point, I have enough light to make it to the next street light. We are able to see just so far spiritually as well. This actually helps us to rely on God, and requires us to exercise the faith that we do have right where we are. A bit like building a foundation with bricks. One brick put into place, and then we are able to place another one, then another. The process takes time and patience, and hard work. Our ONE life purpose is to 'connect with God' and with 'one another'. Aside from all other 'distractions' this is the ONE thing we are created for. Trials and losses, and sorrow cause us to recognize our need for God and for one another. Self-sufficiency actually 'prevents' us from praying and knowing God. "But God who is rich in mercy for His great love wherewith He loved us even when we were dead in sins hath quickened us together in Christ (by GRACE are ye saved) and hath raised us up together and made us sit together in heavenly places in Christ Jesus that in the ages to come he might shew the exceeding riches of his grace in His kindness toward us through Christ Jesus" (Ephesians 2:4-7).

May 21, 2020 Dear (name),

Our dear Grady has found an unwitting accomplice for his outdoor adventures. Seems Mr. B., Audrey's big male cat has figured out how to open the outside screen door at his will! This week Grady was on the porch when Mr. B. decided he was going to go outside and Mr. B. did not want to wait for Audrey to come and open the screen door. Out the door they both went even as Audrey was attempting to prevent that from happening. By the time, I arrived, Grady had been having the greatest time of all. We both went to look for him and spotted him on the bank above our lake. Audrey had been calling him to come, but he refused and ran every time she tried to get close to him. I told her I would go and try to get him. He is not spade yet, and there are other cats in the neighborhood so our concern is 'kittens' from this escape adventure. When I called him, he came running right up to me, and allowed me to just reach down and pick him up! His frequent stair climbing adventures and of longing to come to visit upstairs, netted his quick response to me. Audrey and I looked at each other in amazement. She replied, "Well that was easy!" We both laughed and were both relieved as I handed him to her. Now she had to be extra vigilant to ensure that Grady is not allowed on the porch when Mr. B is out there, as we now KNOW that he can actually open doors! LOL The veterinary clinic will not take him right now, so we have to wait to have him spade, saving their drugs for emergency cases. Such is the COVID19 life!

Our grow light system is now dismantled and all of our plants are now outside. Some planted in the raised bed areas. The tomatoes, peppers and cabbages await being planted in the garden. Fabien wanted them to be 'hardened' to the outside, and we left them in trays so we can move them back inside at night when it is colder here. Fabien put in stakes in our raised beds (again these are cow watering troughs -re-purposed). We can now cover them with a sheet at night – it is still 40'ish at night and we don't want to risk losing the plants.

It is important for us to remember that we are told to live just TODAY. When we start to 'stress' or 'worry' about 'TOMORROW" the Lord asks us to 'redirect' our thoughts. God's promises from the Lord from His Holy

Bible empower us with comfort and assurance during times like these:

"The Lord is good, a stronghold in the day of trouble and He knoweth them that trust in Him" (Naham 1:7). What assurance to KNOW: God Knows! God cares! God IS in control – our world is truly temporary- eternity is FOREVER and EVER! His command is to:

"Continue to grow in the grace and knowledge of our Lord and Savior Jesus Christ" (2 Peter 3:18).

Fight the good fight with ALL thy might!
Faint not nor fear, for He is near,
He changeth not and thou art dear
Life with its way before us lies,
Christ is the way, Christ is the path,
Christ is the PRIZE!

Hymn 'Fight the Good Fight" written by John Monsell (1811-1875).

"For I reckon that the sufferings of this present time are not worthy to be compared with the glory which shall be revealed in us" (Romans 8:28).
"We look for the Savior the Lord Jesus Christ. He is able even to subdue all things unto himself" (Philippians 3:21).

May 28, 2020 Dear (name),

One of our gardens is finally planted outside. We had our friends, Caroline and Adam, come to help us with getting the plants in the ground, so it went faster than what we anticipated. Then Fabien watered everything. After we finished it began to rain so that was perfect timing for what we accomplished. The other garden we will plant from seeds, with cucumbers, squash and potatoes, and I am going to try to grow watermelon this year. We removed all of the blossoms from the blueberry plants. It was hard to do it, but we were told that if we did this next year the plants yield would increase substantially. There were actually not very many berry buds to remove, so it was not a great sacrifice for the promise of a larger yield to come.

We will reach 90 degrees the next few days here. Our insulated drapes keep the heat from coming into our interior home, and this makes a tremendous difference. The ceiling fans help too to keep the air moving which also makes things feel more comfortable.

Fabien worked on the banks that on either side of our 42-step stairway to the boat dock. Quite a job to trim that area because the hill is very steep and tricky to navigate. I used to end up on my backside a few times attempting to do this work with my small weed Wacker. Fabien is stronger and has a bigger machine that really helps in this particular area.

Grady has managed to find another 'hiding place'. Yes, we did not think it was possible, but Audrey uses the cupboard cabinets above her fridge. When she went to pull out bowls stored in that cabinet, she realized Grady was missing again. Because he has discovered that he can follow Mr. B. out he opens the outside screen door, that was the first thing Audrey thought of, that Grady was outside. But then she heard a small 'cat cry' coming from the cabinet above the refrigerator. When she opened the door where the bowls had been located, there was no Grady behind that door, but there was another door to that cabinet, and yes, when she opened that door, there was Grady. He had managed to get himself behind the stack of plates so she could hardly see him, but she could hear Grady and he wanted OUT! Audrey is checking to see if she can get him in to be spaded. Her other two cats spend the night outside. Grady will be able to go outside with the other cats, Mr. B. and Chloe. In the mornings, I find them on my outside deck chair curled up together on the cushion fast asleep with each other, very touching to see for sure.

Our humming bird has found the feeder we put out this past weekend. The leaves are now in full bloom on the trees. A friend of ours is having her backyard leveled and has plants there that we can go and rescue before the bulldozer arrives. We have plenty of space here, and they will be a nice addition to the yard.

Growing seeds from scratch has made me aware of how blessed we are to have food. It takes such effort to grow and a lot of time for it to be ready before we can eat it. That caused me to decide to say 'thanks' for all my food before each meal. Seemed like something that would be quite easy to accomplish. But I am in quite a habit of eating before I say grace, so it is going to take time to get into a new routine for sure. We are encouraged to 'follow after righteousness, godliness, faith, love, patience, meekness" (1 Timothy 6:11). And we are assured that "He heareth the prayer of the righteous" (Proverb 15:29).

Chapter 6

Yesterday: The June Letters

Jesus Christ the same yesterday, to day, and forever.

Hebrews 13:8

In our constantly changing world, it is hard to believe that there is 'anything' that does not change. Yet in the Bible we find that <u>God does NOT change.</u> His promises are true for all those who seek Him with all their heart. Moses wrote in Deuteronomy 7:9: "Know therefore that the Lord thy God He **IS GOD**, the faithful God which keepeth covenant (His promises) and Mercy (undeserved forgiveness) are with them that love Him and keep His commandments to a thousand generations."

Fear is spoken of over 500 times in the King James Version of the Bible. "Fear not" or "Be not afraid" appears 103 times. We cannot live life without encountering events that cause us to fear. The fact that God does not change, provides us with a solid foundation to take our 'fears' to the Lord and to ask Him to provide a way of escape for us. He CAN help us to find a way through the trouble. It is only when we actually 'pray' and 'ask', that God is able to give us a peace that passes our ability to understand. Romans 1:17 encourages us, "The Just shall live by Faith." When we take time to find out God's promises, we can live believing that God has heard our prayer and will answer us in His time. Then we can 'let go' of the fear and just continue to pray and wait. I am always truly amazed when I cry out to the Lord. He is able to help me move forward into the next moment, to just do the next thing, and the next. Before long half my day has passed. His promise from Isaiah 49:29 becomes real for me: "He giveth power to the faint and to them that have no might he will increaseth strength."

THE JUNE LETTERS

June 11, 2020   Dear (Name),

Fabien helped his son, Chad, with raking his hay on the home farm twice this week while Chad used the Hay Baler. Then, Fabien mowed our friend's lawn. Our friends, Caroline and Adam left for CA this week to care for her Dad who is not well. When I returned back home from caring for an elderly man, our place looked amazing. Fabien does things so well. From my office desk I get to watch him do his magic through our French door windows. He works just like a bumblebee' just 'buzzing' around doing this and then that. He went through 3 refills of fuel in his weed wacker machine from doing everything. When I told him, 'I am amazed!", he replied, "I am too! That's a lot of weed whacking!"

I am blessed each morning to hear birds chattering along talking to each other. Fabien and I actually found an owl sitting on a tree along our road. Fabien started to call to the owl, and it flew off, but then we heard another owl call back to Fabien. Yes, Fabien talked for a while with 2 owls and then a 3rd owl, and with Fabien it was 4 owls! It was quite entertaining as we have no idea what he said, and how they responded! The Lord tells us that the hairs on our head are all numbered, so He must be quite the Statistician! Fabien has lost most of his hair on top of his head. He did not 'pull it out' but I know he has had times when he could have done just that!

We have a family of ducks with babies that have been living along a sand dune. Fabien says the Mom takes the babies across the river to the other side and keeps them there, too. He thinks she goes back and forth, moving them to keep them safe from the foxes which we also have here. We have a young deer which started just casually just walking through our back lawn.

Grady did a circuit run yesterday. He is, now, being allowed outside. He went from the lower level and came up to my French door screen off the deck. That door was open as I was watering my plants. He just walked right in like he owned the place! I went and picked him up and carried him to the interior door to the lower level and deposited him there and shut that door. But when I got back into the kitchen, there is Grady again! Right back up from the lower level! He had made a full circle. So, this time I shut the screen door for when he came back. But he didn't come back to the door! Later, I visited with Audrey and she told me she noticed what he was doing too, and she shut her door so he could not go back out! So, Grady got a lesson, of sorts, of what he will not be allowed to do. The Lord has a plan for us as well and our time on earth. Like the 'Ship and its Passengers" Manton says: "Look, as in a ship some sleep, and some walk contrary to the ship's motion, so in the world; some men are negligent, others keep bustling and stirring, and seek to resist the designs of God; but the ship goes on, and the world goes on." Charles Spurgeon elaborates in his book, "FLOWERS" "Yes, a passenger may walk to the north along the deck, but the ship keeps on due south; he may sleep, but the vessel speeds over the waves; he may denounce its motion, but it holds on its way. So, the heathen may rage, and the people imagine a vain thing, but the counsel of the Lord standeth fast forever. Men are free to will and to act but omnipotent wisdom rules over them despite their free agency'. Indeed "Things don't just happen" they are planned by the Lord. As that poem goes, "They are *molded and shaped, and timed by His clock. Things don't just happen; they're planned. We who love Jesus are walking by faith, Not seeing one step that's ahead, Not doubting one moment what our lot might be, but looking to Jesus instead.* "To us who have taken our stand. No matter the lot, the course, or the price, Things don't just happen; they're planned."

Yes indeed, "The Lord reigneth; let the earth rejoice" (Psalm 97:1).

June 18, 2020 Hi (Name),

Our Grady is on the 'mend'. His 'fix' occurred today. He had to go without food and water overnight so he was very hunger and thirsty when my sister Audrey put him into the cat carrier, he worked to claw himself out. They used pain killers, so, he's been sleeping, and his claws were clipped as well. He had begun to 'spray' and that is a smell that is hard to get rid of. He was older than he should have been to have it done, but we now are breathing easier, as we do have a female cat that wanders into our yard, and we certainly don't want kittens.

We have a few strawberries from our garden, very tasty for sure. We added some compost to the plants in our two gardens to help our plants grow. We planted them too early outside, and we are behind the curve of where they should be right now. Some of our friends already have a few tomatoes and we are a very long way away from that. Our summer is also cooler than normal, and that likely is impacting the plants ability to grow. Our poplar trees are shedding and it looks like it is 'snowing' outside as the pollen flies around landing on everything and turning everything 'white' wherever it lands.

The New York Times had a feature article on scientific journals and COVID paper retractions occurring in the leading publications. Fortunately, the three online scientific journals that I process, have not had any retractions. Each has published COVID research articles, reviews, Editorials, and manuscripts. Apparently, I am not the only one that is handling a heavier load. Some Journals are receiving as many as 20 COVID submissions a week. These submissions have to be processed by the ADM's: checked, modified, formatted, etc. for consideration by the Editor for colleague review. Once they get past the gate, typically the colleague review process takes at least 40-45 daysl Most manuscripts require revision which requires more time.

Since March, my computer time has expanded exponentially giving me less time to be outside helping Fabien. Still, I am glad I have the privilege of working from home even if it means dealing with issues here. My printer message this week was, 'ink module almost full'. My brother-in-law removed the ink module and cleaned and replaced it. Apparently, printers have something like a squeegee system that removes extra ink from rollers and deposits it into the ink module. My printer is five years old, and this was my first message. I need the printer for these letters and for the Journal Table of Contents for reference for checking typesetters' final proofs.

Without computers we are limited to pen and paper. David Jeremiah's "Daily in His Presence" Devotional talks about computers: *"Our computer system is truly a marvelous tool. Written in ASCII binary code the zeros and ones give the instructions. The letter "W" is written as 01010111 and the letter "K" is written as 01100001. These are the software codes which are 'binary' - Zero or one: OPEN or CLOSED. Our own life presents opportunities that have 'either/or' choices. Ultimately, we choose: God or not-God. It is in this life that we are given this choice: acknowledge Him or not. Our actions in turn reflect our belief. Choosing to believe in God - it is a 'binary' choice. I have a picture on my kitchen wall that says: "As for me and my House, we will serve the Lord" (Joshua 24:15). Hebrews 11:6 tells us:* "But without faith it is impossible to please him: for he that cometh to God must believe that he is, and that he is a rewarder of them that diligently seek him." In this life we can **see ONLY the 'tip' of the iceberg** – someday we will 'see' the 'rest' of what made everything happen (like the rest of the iceberg under the water). The things that make that 'tip' appear). We will see God – who wrote the code behind it all!

June 25, 2020 Dear (Name),

We have trapped another coon. This one was 22 lbs. Fabien said it was a BIG one! We still have more coming to Audrey's coup to eat seed every night, but Fabien has trapped and released two so far.

We had a bit of 'musical chairs' this week. My sister, Dayle, on my home farm has a bad back and ordered a new better support recliner. She offered her old recliner, that was not so old and in very good shape to us.

Fabien daughter needed a chair, and so we picked up the new chair from the furniture store for my sister, which saved her a delivery charge, and brought it to her home and then removed her recliner and delivered it to Fabien's daughter. We did discuss this move before we ever started, as we knew both of the electric chairs would be heavier than regular chairs. I called a friend of mine, and he told us he would help if he was able to get there in time, and it just happened that he arrived just as Fabien and I were getting ready to pick up the bottom section of her new chair (the heaviest part) to inside the house. So, I was relieved of lifting the chair – Praise His Holy Name for His provision for us with that!

My car just had the winter tires removed and all season tires back on. Everything was closed due to COVID. Then, when I called, they were backed up.

Our 'getting larger by the day', Grady cat, has a brand-new calmer disposition. He has healed from his 'fix' and has a new routine. He arrives every AM at my screen door so he can get back in to go down and eat before Audrey gets back up.

Fabien likes grilled cheese sandwiches, and I made him one this week. I asked him to put together a pot of herbs for a friend of mine, and while he did that, I started to cook his grilled sandwich. After it was done, I took the frying pan off the stove and set it on the sink and went down to see how things were going. When I returned, I realized that the sandwich had continued to cook even though the pan was off the stove. I had left it in the pan to keep it warm, but now it was cold. Fabien arrived and told me, "just microwave it!". Once he saw it on his plate, he smiled. Then he picked up his knife and fork and pulled an 'imaginary' cord on his knife and then proceeded to make a sawing noise with his mouth as he 'cut' his grilled cheese sandwich into small 'crouton' pieces. As he took his first bite, I watched and waited. I said, "You don't have to eat it!" He tasted it and declared, "I think, you are onto something here- You've created 'grilled cheese croutons'! Very crunchy! You need to go on the TV show "SHARK TANK" and sell them!" He had me laughing so hard, I could hardly talk. He truly has an amazing sense of humor. Despite how they looked, he ate most of it - no food wasting here. He gently told me, "Usually it doesn't work very well when you try to do two things at the same time." I told him, "I actually feel just like the cheese sandwich – my day has been 'overdone' too!" I got up late, and then did not feel well, so when I finally started my Journals, I was behind the 'curve' as they say. Then a friend visited who needed help, so by the end of the day, I felt like I had been 'taffy' stretched all day long. The Lord assures us: "My grace is sufficient for thee, for my power is made perfect in weakness" (1 Corinthians 12:9). Sometimes, we must look back to see how that happened. And remember that the PURPOSE of our life is to be 'refined' into a 'vessel' that is without spot or wrinkle, prepared for an eternal home with the Lord in heaven. Our life JOURNEY has an 'end point'. Life is not supposed to be easy. We are indeed not above our Lord, who willing became a 'servant' and our example. My reading this am was in Exodus. Our life is similar to that of the Israelites who had to travel through the 'wilderness' in Egypt 'not knowing', 'not understanding,' having to rely on prayer and the Lord for strength, and courage while we await our own entrance into 'the promised land'. Each 'mess' contains a 'message' that is eternal.

Chapter 7

Today: Be an Eagle! The July Letters

Come unto me, all ye that labour and are heavy laden, and I will give you rest.

Matthew 11:29

We have Eagles that have placed a nest along the waterway where we live. They are truly majestic to watch when they fly above our home. Often, they will dive down to catch a fish! Eagles are one of the birds used in the Bible to encourage us to be patient and willing to wait for the Lord to provide for us. We are told: "Lift up your eyes on high, and behold who hath created these things, Hast though not known? Hast thou not heard, that the everlasting God, the Lord the Creator of the ends of the earth, fainteth not, neither is weary? There is no searching of his understanding, He giveth power to the faint, and to them that have no might he increaseth strength. But they that wait upon the Lord shall renew their strength. They shall mount up with wings as Eagles, they shall run and not be weary, they shall walk and not faint" (Isaiah 40:26, 28, 29, 31). I was told that an eagle can fly above the clouds to avoid a storm when necessary.

We need to live our lives like 'eagles' and get ABOVE our anxieties and fears created by our minds asking those 'What if?" questions. When an issue arises, we MUST stop asking that question and take time to ask God for His help to get through whatever 'it' is.

We are to pray and wait, and work to: "Be ye kind one to another, tenderhearted, forgiving one another even as God for Christ sake hath forgiven you" (Ephesians 4:32).

THE JULY LETTERS

July 3, 2020   Dear (Name),

Hard to believe we are at the July 4 weekend. Fabien's daughter, Celeste, was born on July 4. We won't be doing anything or going anywhere of course, but my plan is to take a few days off from doing the online Journals. That will be a great break for me for sure.

Grady's new pastime is focused on decreasing our chipmunk population. He had to be treated for fleas. Audrey believes he is getting them from the chipmunks. When I picked him up yesterday, he was pretty heavy. He must weigh at least 6-7 pounds now. He is very independent and continues to choose when he wants to sleep, run, play etc. Not too surprising, he is also very interested in birds, but they can fly away.

We have gotten much needed rain this week, which has made our garden look much better. We have determined that what we thought were cabbages, cannot possibly be cabbages. They are tall now and are sprouting seeds. We have no idea what they are. I thought broccoli, but they don't have any broccoli heads at all. Fabien added the wire cages to some of the taller tomato plants to keep them vertical. The lower part of Vermont had flash flood warnings this week, but we were spared all of that heavy rain, and what we got was just a good soaking rain. Our brown lawn is looking greener and better.

Fabien got a weed whacker from his son Chris that doesn't work. It will start but won't continue to run. So, Fabien is working to figure it out, sparkplug, screen, etc. Apparently when they are not run consistently, they plug up.

My cousin, Nancy, sent me a 'serenity' bracelet this week. Its message is perfect for the times in which we live for sure.

God grant me the serenity
To accept the things, I cannot change;
Courage to change the things I can;
And wisdom to know the difference.

Living one day at a time;
Enjoying one moment at a time;
Accepting hardships as the pathway to peace;
Taking, as He did, this sinful world As it is,
not as I would have it;
Trusting that He will make all things right If I surrender to His Will;
So that I may be reasonably happy in this life
And supremely happy with Him Forever and ever in the next.
Amen.
(prayer attributed to Reinhold Neibuhr, 1892-1971)

Am reading a new book entitled, "I did not sign up for this?" All about life's unexpected turns that disrupt our lives. The greatest challenge is to trust that God does have a purpose and not lose faith BUT rather to pray and wait and know that we cannot see eternal things in this physical world. We can only obtain peace by knowing that:

"To everything there is a season, and a time for every purpose under heaven" (Eccelisastice3:1).

THE JULY LETTERS

July 8, 2020   Dear (Name),

Our dear Grady's latest entertainment is hummingbirds as they arrive at our deck feeder. He has found a way to curl up around one of the plants on a stand in the corner. I have removed him from that corner and will block that location to him. I don't want him to disturb the hummingbirds! The turkeys and chickens have created sand pits on our lawn to get cool. Even Grady has decided that is a great spot to cool down in. He gets totally stretched out in the sand. He is very entertaining to watch!

Fabien and I took the canoe to investigate something floating on the water. His fear was it was a dead loon. As we got closer, Fabien said, "It has a rope attached to it." It was a duck decoy. We put it in the canoe and went to visit campers across our lake. As we paddled up, the man came to the shore to greet us with his dog. We talked for a while, and we asked him if he would like to have the decoy for his dog. He replied, "Sure, toss it in the water, he'll fetch it!" Initially, his dog sniffed it as it floated, but wouldn't touch it. His owner walked into the lake to get it and used the string to swirl it around in the air to toss it again into the water. That dog just flew to go get it! It was tossed and retrieved for quite a while before a decision was made to stop. But his dog has a new favorite toy!

We didn't have anyone come for the July 4. We spent time around our fire. The weather was hot so we stayed in the shade. We have one zucchini on a plant. Fabien likes to have them grow to be HUGE. He hollered, "Don't pick it!' I agreed we would let it grow.

Sunday's message was about Zacchaeus the tax collector who climbed up a tree to see Jesus. When Jesus got under that tree he stopped and called him by name to come down. Jesus joined him for supper that night in his house. Tax collectors were not liked by the people. A transformation occurred when the Lord revealed how things looked from 'heaven's perspective' that life is NOT just about THIS current world's riches!
God's word will NOT return void. So, our 'trouble' down here is allowed to get us to 'think' and realize that, indeed, nothing down here is eternal. Here on earth is where we are sifted as wheat from the chaff.
Integrity costs a lot and is the commodity of HEAVEN itself: God is TRUTH, God is LOVE and we have Jesus telling us, "I AM the WAY the TRUTH and the LIFE, no man cometh unto the Father but by me" (John 14:6). "Whosoever shall call upon the name of the Lord -shall be saved" (Romans 10:13).
Psalm 23: "The Lord IS my shepherd - Yea, though I walk through the valley of the shadow of death I will fear no evil for thou art with me, thy rod and thy staff they comfort me. . . and I will dwell in the house of the Lord forever". That is living with eternity in mind.
"Thy face, Lord will I seek" (Psalm 27:8).

Lord I thank you and praise you that you ARE LORD of ALL – past, present and future and nothing is unknown to Thee. You know the END of each thing as well as its beginning and middle. Help us to walk in faith that you have MADE a way for us and HELP US Lord to just take the next step, and the next and the next – please work all the 'bad' for your glory and honor in our lives right now - and for all eternity.

July 18, 2020 Dear (Name),

Fabien's son, Chris, has been staying with us for a few days with his son Garrett, and it has been great to have them with us. They are 'camping' and we have the camper here for them to use. Hard to believe July is half over!!!

We have now gotten several zucchinis now out of the garden. We also had an 'uninvited guest' in the garden last night which was chased out with a broom. A ground hog found our garden. The alert came from the turkeys and chickens which were cackling and running away from the garden fence. Garrett noticed the turkey's making noise and alerted us there was something in the garden! Sure enough, there was! The garden has a wired fence around it, but they are 'well' ground hogs! Fabien located his home under our landing off the stairs that go down to the dock. There is quite a bit of dirt under that landing, so I am quite sure Fabien is correct. Seems once they find a garden they will not stop going back and can eat a row of beans in 30 minutes. We have put a lot of work into the garden so I am sure Fabien will be able to deal with it, even though I hate to think of having to permanently terminate his life, but being able to keep him/them out of a garden appears to be very challenging.

Garrett located the turkey nest. It was on our front lawn fence behind Fabien's hauler. We have not been able to collect any eggs because the hen has been on the nest. The hope is that if we use golf balls the turkey will continue to lay eggs in that nest where we can get them easily. They are pretty good to eat. Fabien does not want to incubate them because it is too late in the season for them to be big enough in the fall to be on their own.

The chicken nest where the chickens are laying eggs is still not located. It's still too hot for the chickens to lay their eggs iin their nests inside the chicken coop, and now that they have a 'spot' outside, they will continue to use it the rest of the summer. The best way is to keep an eye on them and watch where they go, but that takes quite a bit of time, as they are pretty smart and don't want to be seen and will avoid the nest if they know they are being watched.

Deadlines for all 3 Table of Contents for MaryAnn Liebert October issues is July 24, so I am busy this week with those. My work at the law firm last week actually make me feel less 'stressed' with my work on the Journals. Seems sometimes 'comparison stress' has caused me to realize what 'real stress' feels like. At any rate I am happy there was a 'take away' from it that I didn't anticipate.

One of my favorite Bible promises is from Isaiah 42:16: "And I will bring the blind by a way that they knew not; I will lead them in paths that they have not known: I will make darkness light before them, and crooked things straight. These things will I do unto them, and not forsake them."

And 1 Corinthians 14:33: "For God is not the author of confusion but of peace". It is the Providence of God that allows us to be stretched by trials on earth, but it is our Faith that provides us with peace in the midst of our trials, that is not according to our own understanding.

July 24, 2020 Dear (Name),

Read this morning of boy who had a part in a play, and his line that he had to say was, "It is I. Be not Afraid." When it was time for him to say his part, he said, "It's me, And I'm scared!"

We had a 'bee swarm' this week at my sister Treya and Ron's place. By the time we got a bee keeper here, the swarm was gone. The bee keeper told us that when a hive is too small a queen sets out with a bunch of bees to relocate to a new location, and they then form a swarm and send out seeker bees to find a new location and once found they return and bring the queen and all the bees to that new location.

The zucchini plants are producing and I made my first zucchini bread loaves this week from a very large zucchini – that was the size of my lower arm from the elbow down to my hand. Easily made 2 loaves and soup as well. Fabien brought in a yellow squash, a pail of beans, and rutabaga that we grew along with some radishes. Our tomatoes are coming along, all of them are green right now, but we should have some soon. Our lawn has turned back to green from all the rain we received, and our rainwater bins are also full again.

Fabien and I are invited to a memorial service for Roland Chicoque

Luneau in Montgomery on July 25. Fabien was good friends with Chicoque and his wife Ginny. They owned the hotel on the corner of 105 and 78 which was around the corner from Fabien's farm. I met them both last year when Chris was in the hospital, and Chicoque was having problems breathing and he was there for his heart. Our lives on earth are truly for a limited time, and the older I get, the more aware I am of the importance of having FAITH in the work of the Lord Jesus Christ who died for 'us' – me – you – that we may have assurance of ETERNAL LIFE. The only way anything makes sense on earth, is with eternity in view. Most of the time it seems that death is far away and distant. Jesus knew he was going to die. ENOCH and ELIJAH were alive when they were transported to heaven, MOSES and ELIJAH appeared with JESUS on the Mount of Olives with Peter, James and John who saw them as they talked with Jesus about the cross, and then they disappeared – and Jesus alone was left with the disciples. I believe it will be Moses and Elijah who will return to be the witnesses at the wall in Jerusalem during the 7-year Tribulation Period, which occurs after the Rapture of believers from the earth. When Jesus raised Lazareth from the grave after he was dead 4 days, he told Mary: "I am the resurrection, and the life: he that believeth in me, though he were dead, yet shall he live: And whosoever liveth and believeth in me shall never die. Believest thou this? She saith unto him, Yea, Lord: I believe that thou art the Christ, the Son of God, which should come into the world" (John 11:25-27).

"WHOSOEVER shall call upon the name of the Lord shall be saved" (Romans 10:13).

"When my heart is overwhelmed lead me to the rock that is higher than

I" (Psalm 61:2).

'For thy mercy is GREAT unto the HEAVENS and thy truth unto the clouds" (Psalm 57:10).

"When I cry unto thee THEN shall mine enemies turn back – THIS I KNOW for God is for me" (Psalm 56:9).

"For the Lord will not cast off forever, but though he cause grief, yet will He have compassion according to the multitude of His mercies" (Lamentations 3:31-32).

Indeed, the Lord says to us: "It is I. Be not afraid!"

July 27, 2020   Dear (Name),

A friend of mind gave me a box of 'hippo scones' and I found that to be very entertaining! I had someone share with me a poem that is very powerful:

A Friend

A friend doesn't have to be a work of art just to have a heart,

A friend doesn't need to have fur or hair to care,

A friend doesn't have a thing to do but LIKE you,

A friend doesn't need to say a word to be Heard,

It's not so hard to be a friend in the end!

A Humphrey Book by Betty G. Birney

Finally, we have gotten rain and lots of it. Our rain barrels are full again and we have enjoyed not having to water the gardens. The zucchini plants are growing like crazy as well as the yellow squash and beans. The flock's flowers which smell so wonderful are in full bloom here. We have white, pink and deep pink. There are tiny watermelons now on the vine, as well as tiny tomatoes on our plants. We are keeping our eye out for the green tomato slugs that can be so damaging.

My sister, Treya, plans to can several bushels of tomatoes this year as well as beets. We are getting a few tomatoes from our home farm in Georgia, but they don't ripen until much later. The blackberries are going to be great this year! There are tons of them right here close to our property so we don't have to travel very far to pick.

This week when I got up in the middle of the night, I found one of my pillows on the floor next to Fabien's side of the bed. He had just come to bed, so I asked him why he put my pillow on the floor? He replied, "Because it was on 'my' side of the bed, and I didn't want to wake you up – you do sleep with a lot of pillows – so many, that I think I should draw faces on them and tie them to the bottom of the bed! Those pillows make me think of when I would come to bed and find my four kids hogging my side of the bed." I asked, "And what did you do when you found your kids sleeping on your side of the bed?" He replied, "I picked them up very carefully and then carried them to their beds -- they never even woke up!" It was a very touching memory for him to share with me, and entertaining to ponder my pillows with magic marker faces tied to the bottom of our bed. He has quite an imagination and a very funny wit.

Our Grady continues to come every morning to climb up the rail on the deck and stretch as far as he can to get to the hummingbirds that come to the feeder in the morning. Each morning, I have to go out and pick him up off that rail, and tell him that I don't want him to harass my hummingbirds, and then carry him to the door and put him on the top of the spiral staircase to his home downstairs. He is very persistent. He is growing bigger every day.

We are now harvesting turkey eggs now from the turkey's nest under our evergreen bush about two a day. Fabien does not want to incubate them so we will scramble them up and enjoy eating them. My appreciation for 'food' is much greater since I was able to winess the hatching eggs that became 'turkeys' and 'chickens' and 'ducks'. Hearing the 'peep' 'peep' 'peep' as they worked to get themselves free of the shells allowed me to see 'life' in a fresh new way. I will be so happy when we are in eternity when 'death' is no longer present in any form. Such a wonderful, wonderful promise from the Lord to us. His eternal promises for all of us are 'not' so far away! Each promise gives my heart a new level of gratitude for all we have and makes me praise for the Lord for his mercy and grace.

"The wolf also shall dwell with the lamb, and the leopard shall lie down with the kid; and the calf and the young lion and the fatling together; and a little child shall lead them" (Isaiah 65:25).

"And this is the promise that He Himself made to us: eternal life" (1 John 5:11).

"Jesus said, My kingdom is not of this world" (John 18:36).

"For the kingdom of God is not meat and drink; but righteousness, and peace, and joy in the Holy Ghost" (John 14:17).

Chapter 8

Forever: The Rubric Cube: The August Letters

"Enter His gates with thanksgiving and courts with praise: be thankful unto him, and bless his name"

(Psalm 100:4).

Our current world is a bit like one of those Rubric's Cubes. In the beginning when God created everything including Adam and Eve, things were all lined up. All of the different colors of the Rubric's Cube were in perfect harmony. But the one small 'transgression' of Eve and Adam, created a 'disconnect' from dwelling in perfect harmony with God. This began our experience of the results of exercising our 'free will choice." Our choices and make our lives feel like they are twisting and turning just like a Rubric's Cube. To realign with God's Will requires us to make Him the Center of our Will, and to include Him in every thought and deed.
God has promised to realign the entire world when He returns to set up His Kingdom on earth. Jesus uttered the words that assure us of eternal life: "Father, forgive them for they know not what they do!?" (Luke 23:34). We just need to believe and receive like one of the thieves did.

Right now, Jesus says, "If any man will come after me, let him deny himself, and take up his cross and follow me" (Matthew 16:24). As we do this, we will find that our own Rubric's cube of life will begin to align with God's truth. It is through problems, trials, pain, and suffering that we are drawn closer to oneness with God and with one another.

"Wherefore let them that 'suffer' according to the will of God commit the keeping of their souls to Him in well doing as unto a faithful Creator" (1 Peter 4:13).

THE AUGUST LETTERS

August 5, 2020   Dear (Name),

It is when we come to the Lord in humility, knowing the Lord sees very differently than we can, which allows me to say, "Nevertheless, not my will but Thine be done'. This makes it possible for me to move forward even when my prayers are NOT answered as I desire. Certainly, many prayers from true believers are not answered, not because we are not aligned with the Lord within our hearts but, like Paul, we are asked to bear the 'thorns' in our flesh as well while we live on earth in these physical vessels.

Sunday's message was on the importance of 'relationship' and 'prayer' and of appealing to our High Priest in heaven with our requests and then to wait and listen for the Lord to speak to us.

Galatians 4:7: "Wherefore thou art no more a servant, but a son; and if a son, then an heir of God through Christ." The door is WIDE open for us through redemption in Christ to "beg largely" (as Charles Spurgeon says) before our High Priest who abides alive forever more in Heaven with petitions, prayers and supplications. Truly it is the very presence of the Lord that is His great reward to those who seek Him with all their heart, and His presence gives us a comfort that only He can impart -the PEACE in the midst of the STORM! Psalm 145:14: "The Lord upholdeth all that fall, and raiseth up all those that be bowed down." My own goal is to allow Him to say, "My grace is sufficient for thee" (2 Corinthians 12:9).

John Piper on Ephesians 6, "The Weapon Serves the Wielding Power":

"I have been impressed more than ever before that God has given us prayer not as an intercom for increased convenience in our secluded cottages, but as a walkie-talkie connecting the general's headquarters with the transportation line and the field hospital and the frontline artillery. Prayer is not a bell to call the servants to satisfy some desire we happen to feel, it is a battlefield transmitter for staying in touch with the general".

"Take the helmet of salvation and the sword of the Spirit which is the word of God; Praying always with supplication of the Spirit, and watching there unto with all perseverance and supplication for all saints; and for me, that utterance may be given unto me, that I may open my mouth boldly to make known the mystery of the gospel. For which I am an ambassador in bonds; that therein I may speak boldly, as I ought to speak" (Ephesians 6:17-20).

August 6, 2020   Dear (Name),

We are getting a lot of cucumbers, and zucchini squash. I am baking zucchini breads, and making cucumber salads with a sweet onion, mayonnaise and apple cider vinegar delicious. No tomatoes yet, but our watermelons are growing great! And we finally have BROCOLLI!! Picked our first head!

Our friends Carolyn and Adam return from CA this Sunday, so our care for their home, lawn and plants will end this Sunday. They left the end of May to help her father who has cancer. He has pulled thru the treatments and is back home. They may need to return to be there for him again, but it will be great to have them back for sure. We had a lot of rain. Our canoe and the kayaks were lifted and almost taken down river, but Fabien went and removed them from the water. They are being used and not properly put away after being used. So, we will tell people they need to put them back after they use them so we don't lose them.

My sister and her husband have water damage to the wood front and floor in their garage, so the wood needs to be replaced and a new cement foundation made with gravel and drainage in front to prevent damage in the future. Fabien's son Chris has agreed to do the job, and Fabien will help. We got our cement mixer from my home farm yesterday. It is heavy but is on wheels. I asked the Lord to help us load it onto the truck, and when we got there, our friend Bobby showed up just in time to assist Fabien. They created wooden plank rails and just wheeled it right onto the back of the truck! Fabien will use the mixer to fix our cement garage floor too, a project that finally going to be fixed. Praise the Lord! We may be able to cement Audrey's car port area as well, and perhaps Fabien's truck port area.

August 14, 2020 Dear (Name)

We finally are harvesting some tomatoes from our garden. They are small ones, but they are great. We had BLT's last night for the first time here this summer with fresh tomatoes. Fabien continues to unearth gigantic zucchinis the size of half his arm! I have been chopping and parboiling them and freezing them to add to winter soups which are just delicious! Today he brought one in that had stripes on it. It must be a different kind of zucchini that we planted. My sister's Lisa's shipment of garden seeds gave us a great harvest even though the seeds were over a year old. The first cabbage is ready as well, and I am waiting until I can make a large coleslaw for dinner before I pick it.

My sister April's arm will get a cast on Friday. We have had a 'divine solution' to our woodchuck problem. Chris had his wife Bobby bring their dog to visit here, and that dog spotted the woodchuck, and our problem has been solved without us having to do anything at all.

Chris and Fabien have done the repair work to my sister Treya and Ron's garage. The new foundation at the garage came out great, looks like it has always been there. Fabien needs to use his tractor to move more of the gravel away from the entry door so that the drainage of water is going away from that area rather than flowing towards it, but he is very good with doing all of that. He is fun to watch work because he makes the shovel move like it was attached to his 'hand'. And, we have the cement mixer and Fabien has marked with 'white chock' on our garage floor and is getting ready to dig out the damaged cement, so he can pour new cement. Chris made a trough for the cement mixer so that when it is tipped it goes down the shoot into the spot that is framed up.

Sunday's message was on God's 'peace'. "Peace I leave with you, my peace I give unto you, let not your heart be troubled, neither let it be afraid" (John 14:27). This is peace that passes our own ability to 'understand'. Even though the problem still exists, when we pray and 'give things to the Lord' we become like an eagle stretching our minds like 'wings' to bring us above the trouble, above the clouds. And then we can in fact remain 'still' even when the storm continues. This kind of peace must be 'received' through the power of God's Holy Spirit. God's promises in the Bible give us eternity's perspective where 'time' no longer exists as it does on earth. This is the HOPE that is an anchor for our soul which changes the way we 'see' trouble because 'by faith' we can see through 'it' that the Lord can use it to Glorify Himself. Joni Erickson a paraplegic has been successful BECAUSE of her limitations to let people know that the Lord is not limited by limitations. Nick Vujicic, born without arms or legs, says he is ironically happier than most people who have arms and legs. He married Kanae and they have 2 boys and twin girls. His life is inspirational because he focuses on what he 'has' and not on what he doesn't' have' and is grateful rather than bitter or anger. He admits that life is very challenging, but has given his life to the Lord, and looks for the miracles daily as they acknowledge the very presence of the Lord in the midst of each trial, BECAUSE God has promised to work it 'all' for our good. This is truly an ANCHOR for me! I tell the Lord all the time, "USE THIS – for your glory – or WORK THIS for your good! Some of which we will not see how God did that, until we are on the other side. Therefore, we all have a LOT to look forward to, as we make those divine FAITH deposits into Eternity which is better than a bank.

"Which hope we have as an anchor of the soul, both sure and steadfast" (Hebrews 6:19).

Grady continues to bless and entertain us. He catches flies! Yes, he spots them, and is like a pointer dog, he is still when he sees one, and then faster than a fly swat, he jumps and eats it! And he rarely misses! He can jump very high!

August 20, 2020 (name)

Fabien is harvesting the gardens every night and brought in two whopper big tomatoes last night. April got her final cast on her arm is doing so much better. Amazing how our bodies can heal like that! Fabien finished moving the gravel in front of my sister Treya and Ron's garage to divert the water AWAY from the front of the entry to that garage. He added pipe drainage in front of the door, as well as created a trench for water run off further away to ensure the water has a place to go rather than just sit there in the ground and cause problems for the new foundation.

Last week was quite amazing. I had a hair appointment and called my friend to see if I could drop by outside to bring her a book. She agreed she would meet me outside so I headed her way. On my way up the driveway up to the house, I really felt like my friend, SueBee was right there with me. And I began to think about my friend SueBee and how amazing it was that I was even going to see my new friend. I began to talk out loud to SueBee in my car. I told her how amazing it was that had it not for our close friendship, I would not be visiting m new friend and then I told her I would see her 'soon' (in the sense that I know my eternal destination is with Jesus in heaven- having put my trust in His work on the cross for me). After me and my friend had visited, later that day, she texted, "Did you know it is SueBee's birthday today?" And, of course, I did not know THAT at all. So, we both got a sense of SueBee's 'presence' with us on her birthday! The last time I chose to do 'something' unwittingly on someone's birthday was at UVM. I arrived at work early and decided to weed under the memorial bench put outside Votey Hall for Dr. Jean-Guy Beliveau. As I finished that early morning, the head of the custodial crew said, "Is that how you start you days now, Dawn – weeding under a bench? – don't you know we have people 'here' to do that?!" I replied, "I know, but do YOU know whose bench this is that I was weeding under?" He had no idea. So, I told him about Dr. Beliveau being my friend who had passed about 2 years earlier and that the bench was in his memory and that he was in heaven, as I handed him a Bible book in memory of Dr. Beliveau. Later that morning, I left my office and went past the Dean's Office entrance, just as someone came out the entrance door, and Sharon the receptionist yelled out to me and asked me to come into the Dean's Office. When I did, she asked, "Did you know Jean-Guy is in the Burlington Free Press (BFP) today?" I replied, "He can't be, he's dead!" She said, "I know, but he IS in the BFP. I replied, "You'll have to show me!" She handed me the BFP and there was his big smiling face – his family has put a memorial in the BFP in honor of his birthday that very day in his memory. I went back to my office and called his wife, Connie, and told her and she invited me to their camp in Swanton. After work I went to the camp, and got to visit with his grandkids and be part of their birthday celebration in his honor. My heart is full of gratitude and praise on how amazing God really is moments like these that give us assurance that those things that are written in the Bible are indeed true!

This past Saturday I was praising God even though I was having problems. I told the Lord, "I am going to just 'wait' for this to issue to come to an end - however long that takes!" Then, that afternoon we had a freak rain storm pass through Highgate and when that storm was over a 'rainbow' appeared over our lake here! For me, that rainbow was confirmation from the Lord that HE heard my praise, and that there was indeed a 'rainbow' of His blessing coming our way.

"My grace is sufficient for thee for my power is made perfect in weakness" (1 Corinthians 12:9).

August 28, 2020   Dear (Name),

Fabien added 'chicken' eggs to the nest that the turkey hen is nesting on. She has 1 turkey egg, one golf ball, and around 10 chicken eggs. The chicken eggs should hatch on Sept. 11 along with the turkey egg, as the chicken eggs were added just about a week after she started laying on the nest. We will have things in reverse from Sue Irish's where her chicken hatched turkey eggs and those 2 turkeys still follow that chicken around. It is the most entertaining thing to see. The turkeys roost above her head on a pole that John added for them -- full grown turkey hens. Their father Tom and mother turkey hen are in the yard but the hatched turkeys continue to remain with the chicken. So, we are pretty sure the turkey will adopt the chickens as well.

It is cooler and days are darker morning and night. We are working to be ready for winter here. We still have several weeks to go with the gardens. The watermelons and melons are quite nice this year. We finally got quite a lot of broccoli heads, and cabbages. The picked garden veggies taste sweet without any bitterness.

There are some maple trees beginning to turn colors here and there along Route 207 to Highgate Center and on Route 78 to Swanton. I am so thankful I am not working at UVM. With COVID19 some classes are being provided in the UVM CEMS labs. Students have to agree to wear masks to be on campus, but many have 'off campus' housing. We remain very careful and are still not going places. My grocery shopping is once a month and I am now used to doing that.

Sunday's message was on the Kingdom of God that is to come. He began with the verse "God is true" (John 3:3). The most interesting numbers are 3:3 - the first 3 represents the 'trinity" (3) the second 3 represents the mind, heart and soul of man – (3) which creates a perfect alignment. Similar to still water reflecting a perfect image of the shoreline. The wonderful thing is when we intentionally 'align' our heart and mind, we 'see' divine things. There is not enough 'consecration' and 'separation' of our mind and heart toward God. Our world is too full of earthly distractions that 'call us' away from God. Quite a bit like Grady, who still has no time for being picked up and held and petted. He has things to do, and places to go – and my attention is for him a big interruption to his already busy schedule. He is my example of what not to be like with the Lord! This morning I got up an extra hour early, so I had a wonderful time reading the Bible, and searching for parallel verses and just reading them and repeating them and thinking about them. When I was done, I took my key verse: "Hear, me when I call O Lord, have mercy on me" (Psalm 4:1); and typed it up and as I typed, it, I said the verse right out loud to the Lord and I really meant it from my heart to the Lord's heart – very intense and sincere request -and as soon as I finished saying those words, the kitchen door that was closed ajar – had a gust of wind come and blow so hard it pushed the door WIDE OPEN - instantaneous – and delightful, I began laughing out loud and exclaimed, "Well, Lord, I KNOW you heard me – I see your Holy Spirit has come right in!"

"Life without God is like an unsharpened pencil - - NO POINT.

Living Life for God is THE POINT!

John the Baptist proclaimed,

"Behold (look) the lamb of God who takes away the sins of the World" (John 1:29).

We need to be

INTENTIONAL –

FOCUSED –

like Esther, Nehemiah, Jesus, Elijah

Each was INTENTIONAL.

The more of the Bible promises we have within us, the more linked we become to the Lord and to one another.

How incredibly GREAT is that?!

Chapter 9

FAITH Waits: The September Letters

But yield yourselves unto God, as those that are alive from the dead, and your members as instruments of righteousness unto God.

Romans 6:13

When it seems that God is silent to our cries, we must exercise faith in God. We must: Pray and Wait. The key is to KNOW that God **IS** in control of ALLl things and has promised to work ALL THINGS for good to them that are called according to His purpose (Romans 8:28)t. He WILL provide answers to all of our questions – in **_HIS_** time!

Habakkuk is a good example of someone who did not understand what God allowed to happen. But in the end, Habakkuk decided to walk by FAITH and not by SIGHT. "I will stand upon my watch, and set me upon the tower, and will watch to see what he will say unto me, and what I shall answer when I am reproved" (Habakkuk 2:1). The Lord did answer him: "And the Lord answered me and said, "Write the vision, and make it plain upon tables, that he may run that readeth it, for the vision is yet for an appointed time, but at the end it shall speak and not lie: though it tarry, **_WAIT FOR IT_** because it will surely come. It will not tarry" (Habakkuk 2:2-3).

It was shepherds in the field who witnessed the sky light up with a host of angels that proclaimed, "Fear not, for behold I bring you good tidings of great joy which shall be to ALL people. For unto you is born this day in the city of David a Savior which is Christ the Lord" (Luke 2:10-11). God's plan for this earth is right on track. Nothing is beyond His purpose. Nothing is beyond His control. "For in Him we live and move and have our being" (Acts 17:28).

THE SEPTEMBER LETTERS

September 5, 2020 Dear (Name)

Well, we have finally gotten a few apples off one of our trees! The birds have apparently tasted them as there are some holes on them, but we can cut that off. I am happy to have any at all! Our windows have to be shut at night now as it is getting too cold to keep them open, as the pellet stove will be 'kicked on' and we don't need to have that running this early. Fabien and I have visited Chris in Richford and he is coming along with fixing the roof and wall of the addition on his home where the stove will be located. He got the rotten wall off, and has put up new plywood. The cost for plywood has gone from $8 to $23 a sheet. We could hardly believe the price is so high, but COVID has shut down plants and the stores cannot get supplies right now. Chris had to finish putting up half of the roof with plywood and steel. This is a 'utility room' for his freezer and storage area for his furnace. Chris and Bobby have a 'blue yeller' dog that just loves to run. He begged and begged for me to throw his 'toy' and once that game started, he was persistent to keep it going! I even got Fabien to toss the 'toy'. The dog is truly entertaining to watch as he deliberately runs much further than where the toy falls, just for the 'joy' of running. Chris's two pigs were rendered and we got half of one of them and that is being processed. They are pretty happy that taking care of those pigs is over. This has been a lot of work added to their already full day. Fabien and I had 3 pigs for just one month, so we know firsthand how much work it is to keep them watered and fed daily. Fabien did the work most of the time, but I was asked to care for them now and again. I am happy to know that we can do that here, but glad that we are not doing that in addition to the gardens.

Our turkey hen is a 'lesson' in patience and persistence. She is diligently sitting quietly on her nest, day in and day out. Fabien thought she was 'dead' the other day, and so he gently reached into the evergreen bush and gently pulled one of her tail feathers to see if she would move. He told me she quickly lifted up her head. So, she is very much alive and well there. She was soaking wet though! We had a very heavy storm with lots of rain, and that bush she is setting under is no able to keep her dry. She has Audrey's chickens and they come and lay down around and under that same bush. The Tom turkey also comes and just hangs around all the time. So, it is a regular 'circus' with all sorts of animal activity going on as that hen turkey 'sits' there very still. Seems the animals are aware of 'holy ground' with nesting is happening. You would think humans would know the value of those that are yet 'unborn' -too.

Chris now has a 'sponsor'. Fabien has reminded me that this work is a marathon, and not a 'sprint' and that it is going to take time for Chris to work his way out of addiction. It has been quite a roller coaster ride for everyone involved. The goal is to remain in the 'present' and work to make each day the best that it can be. Like 'Abraham who believed God and it was counted unto him for righteousness" (Romans 4:3)' ". . who against hope – believed in "HOPE" (Romans 4:18). "He staggered NOT at the promises of God through UNBELIEF but was STRONG IN FAITH GIVING glory to God" (Romans 4:20). "Being fully persuaded that what He (GOD) had promised, HE (GOD) was able to perform . . and therefore, it was imputed to him for RIGHTEOUSNESS" (Romans 4:22). Abraham was actually called 'the friend of God" (James 2:24). I am feeling much like Abraham, and I am having to walk in faith just like Abraham, who said, "My son God, will provide Himself a lamb for a burnt offering' so they went both of them together" (Genesis 22:8).

And so, we go with the Lord walking together in FAITH and in HOPE and WAIT like our Turkey patiently and persistently for God's perfect time for answered prayers. Again, in FAITH, waiting. Patiently waiting.

September 10, 2020 Hi (Dear Name),

We got a ton of rain and it knocked over Chad's crop of hemp plants. Fabien went to help pound wooden stakes into the ground and prop up as many plants as they could. It is still two weeks to harvest time. Some hemp plants are as large as small Christmas trees. This back breaking work has been done for 2 days now and today will be the 3rd day. Certainly, worth doing, just not easy to do.

The trees are turning colors now and we hope to take a drive up to the Newport area, as those leaves turn first. We planned to do the trip this week, but the work needed for the hemp crop, trumped our trip. My own work on the Journals has kept me busy this week, as I did not process any papers during the Labor Day weekend. Whenever I miss a 'day' the papers just pile up in the cue and sit there waiting for me to process. It was great to have a few days off for sure.

My oldest sister Carol will move this week from MA back to VT. She is going to be taking our Grady as her new cat, so we are going to miss him for sure. When Audrey took Grady in, she already had two cats and the older Tom cat and Grady have been getting into 'battles' for territory here. Her Mr. B. cat is seeking refuge at my sister's Treya's home, but she already has a cat. My taking Grady doesn't solve anything because we are living where Mr. B. lives, so Grady and him would continue to go 'at it' with each other for dominance. We have seen happen here with the male turkeys and had to 'give away' and relocate our Tom hen – that is how John and Sue ended up with our Tom turkey and with her chicken hatching that Tom's turkey eggs. This is the weekend that we expect to have our turkey hatching chicken eggs as well as a turkey egg. We will see how it goes.

Sunday's message was on the book of Acts and how answered prayers are often different than we expect. Miraculous answers to our prayers are wonderful when thy occur. But quite often we are right where Jesus was when we are praying for our 'deliverance'. "Father, if thou be willing remove this cup from me, nevertheless not my will but Thine be done (Luke 22:42). Even Paul was left with a 'thorn in his flesh' by the Lord despite his plea to have it removed. This often brings me to the place where I have to cry out, "Lord I believe help thou my unbelief" (Mark 9:24). Our walk of FAITH requires that we indeed not JUDGE things before the time, but rather that we willing, patiently wait, as we 'Cast our care upon Him" knowing that "He careth for you" (1 Peter 5:7).

The older I get, the more aware I am of how little we 'truly understand' regarding what is allowed to occur while we are on earth. We are encouraged that "The effective fervent prayer of a righteous man availeth much" (James 5:16). Prayer is where true FAITH is discovered. Quite often we are like King David who exclaimed: "My soul melteth for heaviness, strengthen thou me according to thy word" (Psalm 119:28). When we get to the other side in heaven, when that curtain is pulled back, THEN we will 'understand' the why's behind all the trials. Right now, we are encouraged to know that the Lord is aware of all of them. He assures us: "Blessed are the undefiled in the way who walk in the law of the Lord. Blessed are they that keep His testimonies and that seek Him with the whole heart (Psalm 119:1&2). Now, I can pray: "Lord I will keep thy statutes, O forsake me not utterly" (Psalm 119:8), because I know: "Surely there is an END and thine expectation shall not be cut off (Proverbs 23:18).

"Eye hath not seen, nor ear heard, neither have entered into the heart of man, the things which God hath prepared for them that love him" (1 Cor. 2:9).

September 16, 2020 Dear (Name)

Our expected 'baby chickens and baby turkey' did not arrive. The eggs that the turkey hen was nesting over, were all rotten. It was past 21 days and my sister Audrey encouraged us to get her off the nest Fabien pulled on her tail to get her to turn around. She was head in, so Fabien had to get her to turn around to get her out. She bit his finger. There was no blood as she did not break his skin. Fabien got the eggs out and checked each of them, all rotten. His pants were so smelly from that job, he had to change them and I had to wash them right away! That hen kept going back to the nest, so Fabien put a piece of wood on top of the nesting spot.

I got water and grain and grit to entice her to eat. But she was not interested. The other turkeys, rooster and chickens were excited to get an extra banquet. When Fabien went to walk to the compost area, that turkey hen flew right at him. He told me he was scared she was coming to attack him, but she landed right next to him and just walked around him. He felt she was actually flying because she was happy to be 'off the nest' and able to get her life back! It is sad that there aren't any baby chicks, but we are happy we saved the hen. Audrey says the hen could have died nesting. Seems hens won't stop nesting and some die nesting. So, we saved our turkey hen's life!

Our trip to help Chris with his house room roof went well. Chris used pieces of steel he had leftover. We were able to help with other projects too: moving a wood pile to open up their driveway for winter plowing, and moving his truck rack and canoe into storage for the winter. Fabien stabilized the entry deck floor, and I did dishes and cleaned inside. Things are always a lot less like 'work' when you are doing things together. Our plan is to go at least once a week to help him and his wife Bobbie out.

Our melons and watermelons are ripe and we are eating them! They are quite good. Neither of us thought we could grow them here, BUT then what do we know? We had NEVER tried!

We just watched a Documentary movie called, "Harry & Snowman". Harry deLeyer was an immigrant from Holland who came to America. He and his wife had 8 children. His father raised horses, so he got a job working for a horse farm. He decided he would go to the auction to see if he could get a horse for a small amount of money. He arrived too late, as they were loading 'unwanted' horses onto trucks to go to the glue factory. Harry looked and saw a white 'work' horse on a truck and asked if he could buy him. He got him $80 and called him 'Snowman"! His kids used Snowman as a diving board because the horse liked to swim. Harry had promised to sell the first horse he got to his neighbor for their daughter. Snowman was the first horse that was good with kids, so he sold Snowman. But Snowman came back 3 days later, and continued to return again, and again. They put a tire on his leg and put a high fence around his area. But Snowman came back with the tire on his hoof. So, the man sold him back to Harry! Harry promised Snowman that he would never sell him again. Then, Harry decided to ride Snowman to see how high he could jump. He was a workhorse with big feet, but he could jump! Snowman ended up winning three Triple Crowns of Jumping and won every race he was entered in for 10 years. Harry and Snowman traveled the world making history. Snowman set a new record for the high jump that lasted for 10 years. Snowman would even jump over other horses. The horse was totally yielded and obedient. Harry let him retire and then finally had to put Snowman down, then, ten years later on a different horse, Harry the Master of training horses, won another Triple Crown of Jumping! Christ as our Master and He too is able to help us jump over the obstacles put in front of us when we are yielded and obedient!

September 25, 2020 Dear (Name)
Well, Fabien has cleaned out one garden. We got about 25 potatoes this year, a pretty sad yield, but well we only planted a few potato plants rather than an entire garden full of them. We got a few more small yellow squash and a small zucchini. Now that 'garden' area is dirt for next year.

I had never heard of this being done, but Fabien used old oil to 'paint' his utility shed to preserve the wood. It looks 'black' once it is done, but Fabien says the color will brighten as time goes on. He explained that is not really 'painting' as the oil just drips off of the brush when it is turned upside down on the boards. He used the brush around to move the oil into the boards. It was pretty smelly, so I didn't get too close as 'chemical smells' are toxic to my body.

Our pellet stove is kicking on at night as temps get below 60 degrees. We are protected by being close to the water from freezes. Chris in Richford has had at least 2 hard freezes and their garden did not survive the second freeze, it killed everything - tomatoes, squash and zucchini. Fabien has been working to continue to get us ready for winter here. The canoes and kayaks are out of the water and put away. I brought plants inside to ensure they were not killed by cold temps.

Hard to believe but September has just flown by, and October is next week. Our weekend with Dave for respite went very well. We travelled with him to Chris's in Richford to bring him a wheelbarrow Fabien fixed for them, and some wood, and 4 stools for the new island he made in their kitchen. The colors are turning more and more, so we are headed into our full foliage season.

My hope is to start making my books into Audio books. I have been told that my new computer has the capacity to do the recording. My brother-in-law is willing to help me get it set up to do it. Fabien has agreed that the best time will be at night between 8 and midnight, that is when it is the quietest outside and there can be no background noise. This will be my next challenge. I did record one book in audio format, but ACX refused it because the recording had 'pops'. I was told to re-record it but I did not have the right equipment then, so I did not feel I could do any better than I had already done. Hopefully this time I will have success.

My anchor verse this week has been: "Fear thou not for I am with Thee, be not dismayed for I am Thy God. I will strengthen thee, yea, I will help thee, yea I will uphold thee with the right hand of righteousness" (Isaiah 41:10).

I am learning to be more grateful for 'health' and to make my main desire each day to be 'to be pleasing in His sight." Sat. Sept 26 had a rally in Washington DC entitled, "Return to Me", by Johnathan Cahn. Franklin Graham and Pastor Cahn scheduled 28 speakers with messages related to the times in which we live. Someone told me today, that life itself is a 'course' that most of us are unaware that we are enrolled in, designed to help us deal with the trials that arrive for each of us. Life's purpose is to prepare us for eternity, but this fact seems to escape our minds as we work to get through each day. "Knowing this, that the trying of your faith worketh patience. But let patience have her perfect work, that ye may be perfect and entire, wanting nothing" (James 3:1-4).

It is of comfort to know that BELIEVERS in Jesus Christ cannot 'lose'. Everything God allows, brings fresh insights that are designed to transform us into His image.

Chapter 10

Let Good Overcome Evil: The October Letters

If therefore thine eye be single, thy whole body shall be full of light.

Matthew 6:22

There is a Christian hymn that says: "Every promise in the book is mine, every chapter, every verse, every line". There is only one way to overcome evil with good and that is God's way, through God's love. In truth, the love that the Lord has for each of us, is indeed as though there were only 'one' of us. We are instructed: "Trust in the Lord with all your heart and lean onto our OWN understanding; in all thy ways ACKNOWLEDGE HIM and HE WILL direct thy paths" (Proverbs 3:5). It is up to us to make our 'eye' single. That can occur when we obey His commands in the Bible.

His Commands:
"And be not confirmed to this world but be ye transformed by the renewing of your mind that ye may prove what is that good and acceptable and perfect will of God" (Romans 12:2).

"Let us therefore come boldly unto the throne of grace that we may obtain mercy and find grace to help in time of need" (Philippians 4:16).

"For we have not a high priest which cannot be touched with the feelings of our infirmities but was in all points tempted like as we are yet without sin" (Hebrews 4:15).

"Abide in me and I in you. As the branch cannot bear fruit of itself except it abide on the vine no more can ye except ye abide in me" (John 15:4).

"But the fruit of the Spirit is love, joy, peace, longsuffering, gentleness, goodness, faith, meekness, temperance, against such there is no law" (Galatians 5:22-23).

"This then is the message which we have heard of Him and declare unto you that God is light and in Him is no darkness at all" (1 John 1:5).

"But if we walk in the light as He is in the light we have fellowship with one another and the blood of Jesus Christ His son cleanseth us from all sin" (1 John 1:7).

"He giveth power to the faint and to them that have no might He increaseth strength" (Isaiah 40:29).

PRAYER: Lord, we need the presence of your Holy Spirit to guide us. Please intervene and help us to seek your will, to be willing to wait and then be obedient to your leading. Help us to remember:
"Kindness is the language that the deaf can hear and the blind can see".
Mark Twain

THE OCTOBER LETTERS

October 9, 2020 Dear (Name)

Summer flew by, and Fall has arrived. Fabien has cut back all of our Hosta plants around the house, garage, trees, and firepit area, as the leaves are falling off the trees. Our deck chairs and cushions are now under cover as well. Most of the corn has been harvested. We continue to make trips to help Chris in Richford with getting the stove hooked up inside his home.

Northside Church has started their Sunday night Kids program, and Adult Bible study at that same time for parents. This Sunday was the first session. Pastor Dan is doing 1 Peter. The apostle Peter is actually a lot like us in many ways. His confidence actually worked against him many times. He is the disciple who gave the correct answer to Jesus's question, "Who do men say that I am?" when he declared, "Thou are the Christ the Son of the living God!" He also was quick to step out of the boat during a storm when Jesus walked on water, only to find himself sinking and reaching out for the Lord's hand before going under. Peter was the one that swore he would never deny the Lord, then Jesus told him he would that very night, deny him 3 times before the rooster crowed once. Peter was the one who cut off the ear of Malcus when the guards arrested Jesus in the garden, only to have Jesus touch and heal Malcus's ear. Peter also was the one who got tired of 'waiting' for the Lord and declared to the other disciples "I go a fishing!" upon which all of them followed him to the fishing boat! The disiples, after being out all-night fishing and catching nothing, then saw the Risen Lord Jesus Christ on the shore with 'coals' of fire and fish thereon, shouting to them to: "Cast your net on the right side of the boat" whereupon they caught the famous 153 fish. The number 153 is a fixed, constant and unchangeable number that catches one-third of all numbers with multiples of three (trinity) and with quantities under 2000. – James Harrison "The Pattern and the Prophecy"). Jesus then told Peter 3 times to: feed my lambs x1, and feed my sheep x2. Peter then responded with a question and asked, And what will this other disciple be asked to do? Jesus then rebuked him for being a 'busy' body rather than focusing on what he was asked to do.

I see my own life superimposed over Peter's with my own level of confidence that has surprised me when things didn't go the way I'd planned. My own zeal, like Peter's causes me to jump ahead of the Lord with great faith, only to find that I need to cry out to Him for His help when I find myself sinking fast. My own impatience making me spin my wheels and causes me to also accomplish nothing spiritually.

So, it was with great interest that I listened to Pastor Dan talk about the book that Silvanus wrote on behalf of Peter. Silvanus was one that walked with the Lord Jesus Christ for 3 years. Peter wrote his letter to the 'Elect" of God, who are sanctified (set-apart for His use). He declared us to be 'strangers' and pilgrims in this current world. 1 Peter 1:2 contains the Trinity: '<u>God the Father</u>, through sanctification of <u>the Spirit</u>, unto obedience and <u>sprinkling of the blood of Jesus Christ</u>. Peter prays that "GRACE" (unearned favor) and "PEACE" (undeserved forgiveness) be 'multiplied' to us.

When each day seems to bring us more 'bad news', we can thank Peter for a message that contains inner peace: We are NOT alone! God's Holy Spirit is with us! God's promises are true! We have an inheritance incorruptible and undefiled that fadeth not away reserved in heaven (1 Peter 1:4).

God is not looking for 'perfection' from us. God knows we need His help. He asks us to EXERCISE the FAITH we have, take the next step, even when it is hard to do, KNOWING someday we WILL meet Jesus, as well as Peter and all the disciples, and all the other people when we reach our eternal perfect home! It is my prayer that you are comforted today by these promises as well!

October 15, 2020 Dear (Name)

We have had a few beautiful days here, and have gotten the rain that we needed! This week, Fabien has installed some ceiling lights in his outdoor garage extension area. He also came into the garage just as I beginning to back my car out. I stopped and looked as he stood and jumped with his arms out! I rolled down my window to find out what he wanted. His reply, "Look behind you!" Well, the garage door had 'closed' on me, and I had not realized that had happened! I was just about to back right into it! I shut my car off and went and gave him a hug and thanked him. He didn't even know what he had come into the garage to get. Certainly, the Lord had 'guided' him to be there to prevent me from backing into the door. He told me he wasn't sure I would be able to stop in time. I was less than an inch away from hitting the door when I stopped. Certainly, in the realm of 'miraculous'. When I opened the garage door, it opened. But when I walked around the back of the car, my purse must have triggered the lights that caused the door to begin to close. But I did not realize that the door had turned directions on me. Because I had seen the door open, I started to back up when that door was actually on its way back down. This type of 'excitement' is something we can readily do 'without' in life. Truly I have had an 'attitude of gratitude' this week for sure!

Fabien's hunting trip begins this weekend. He will travel to PA with his cousin to their hunting camp for a week, and another friend will join them. The last time they went hunting, they watched as a bear came and stole a bag of 'meat' from a deer that they had shot from off the porch of the motor home in the middle of the night. It makes me glad that he is there with two other experienced hunters. My role is to prepare a potato salad and a meatloaf for him to bring with him. It is quite a drive, about 10 hours from here. But that is, of course, part of the FUN of the trip! I also have a 'respite weekend' with our friend Dave who will come Friday night and remain with me through Sunday night.

All of the above, is a reminder of the importance of living 'in the moment' in which we are 'in'. To just be 'all in' with whatever task we are assigned to do no matter how routine. And we are told to DO 'that' all to the glory of God! Whether brushing our teeth, washing our face, combing our hair, etc. – God is there with us – in each and every moment! We truly miss out on fellowship with him when we focus on 'where we are going' rather than 'in the moment we are in'. Being and staying in the 'moment' in which we are in is the 'key' to being aware of the eternal presence of the Lord with us: EMANUEL: God with us!

"Thou wilt keep him in perfect peace whose mind is stayed on thee because he trusteth in Thee" (Isaiah 26:3). The song, "I Sing the Mighty Power of God" by Isaac Watts 1674-1748 says:

"And everywhere that man can be, Thou, God, art present there." This is very comforting to know. Isaac Watts penned 750 Christian hymns, but loved making rhymes like:

"A little mouse for want of stairs ran up a rope to say its prayers."

Truly we need to 'go out of our way' to ensure that we make 'time' each day to 'pray' even when our regular mode of access i.e., the 'stairs' of ease to pray have been taken away. And when unexpected trouble, sorrow or loss arrive, that is when we truly bring glory and honor to our Creator when we still PRAY! It is 'those HARD times' from life that secure eternal RICHES and REWARDS. These will be made known to us when we arrive to our ultimate HEAVENLY destination! Won't that be: 'Just out of this world'! No wonder we will proclaim:

"Saying, Amen: Blessing, and glory, and wisdom, and thanksgiving, and honour, and power, and might, be unto our God for ever and ever. Amen" (Revelation 7:12).

October 21, 2020 Dear (Name),

Fabien's hunting trip has been quite exciting already this year. Seems one of the three shot a buck and headed out with their four-wheeler to pick it up. They located it beside a big fallen tree. Harris grabbed the rack on the deer which was very large, think it was a 12 pointer, and picked the head up and touched its eye to see if it was dead. Fabien was on the other side of the deer and saw the other eye move. He told Harris. "The deer is alive!" Just then, the deer decided it was time to 'get out of there' and got up and ran away. Seems they grazed the back leg on it but not enough to do much damage. None of them had rifles with them, because they were sure the deer would be dead. The next morning Fabien headed to his tree stand with his muzzle loader and watched 2 large Bucks come and stand right under him. His license is for a 'doe' using his muzzle loader, so he could not shoot either of them. But he got to watch them move around in close range. They have gotten so many deer over the years, that is the true accounts of events like these that have 'true story telling power'.

I have taken on filling three Samaritan's Purse Shoebox s for Christmas. Northside Church does about 400 of them each year. We were asked to take the shoe boxes and fill them and return them to the church. The church will then mail them to Samaritan's Purse which will fly them to missionary destinations around the world. The wonderful part of the project is that they ask that people who create the gift boxes place a personal note inside the box for the child that receives the box. This project opens the door for me to work with some children that I know to have them place something within a box that is 'from them' to another child around the world that is the same age. This should provide a way of connecting with a new friend for each of them.

There has been a missionary speaker this week who has delivered very powerful messages related to how we live our lives. He asked us, "What was the most quoted verse in the Bible?" I thought it would be John 3:16 "For God so loved the world that He gave His only begotten Son that whosoever believeth in Him should not perish but have everlasting life." But that was NOT the most quoted verse. That would be Matthew 7:1 "Judge not, that ye be not judged." He went on to explain how this "Judge not" verse is used incorrectly in our world and taken out of context. The Lord who had just finished the Sermon on the Mount, had gone on to provide further instructions for how to not be a hypocrite. The message was powerful. In the end, those who judge receive back the very judgment as they have judged. We are to examine ourselves when we feel a need to condemn because it is very likely that we will need to pull out the 'beam' that is in our own eye, and that will enable us to assist with removing a 'small twig' from theirs. The intent of Christ's messages were for reconciliation and not for using commandments without love and care. The commands are to draw us to one another and to God's love, and forgiveness.

The second message he gave was on stress. Our Expectations VS Our Reality is what creates stress. Our anxiety will take our Reality and add to that those 'What if" possibilities. When we walk in fear, depression arrives, and that produces a sense of Hopelessness. It is "Compartmental Depression" that we experience due to unresolved issues. Elijah in 1 Kings 19:4 said: "It is enough!" He was so depressed, that he just wanted to just die. He left town and went and isolated himself which made things even worse. God sent and Angel to Elijah to give him food to eat and then encouraged him to rest. It is staying in touch with others and caring for our physical needs and eating and sleeping properly that helps us to recovery from stress. An angel was sent to help and that angel did not deny or minimize the situation, but did correct him and told him he was not alone and that God is indeed in control of ALL things. After he was rested, God instructed Elijah to 'go' and do another assignment. So, it is being in touch with God and with others that enables us, like Elijah, to regain HOPE! And HOPE maketh us not ashamed (Romans 5:5). None of us know the future, we are to live our best 'today'.

October 29, 2020   Dear (Name),

It is GREAT to have Fabien back home! Because of COVID, he didn't make any stops on his way home, so it was a long drive. Then the undoing of the unpacking began the next day. The fallen leaves here were almost a foot deep in our back yard, so leaf cleanup has begun. Fabien used his zero-turn rider mower to blow the leaves into HUGE piles. These piles can be picked up with his tractor bucket using his wooden box extender he created for the tractor bucket. That holds about 5 wheelbarrow loads of leaves, so it makes things go a lot quicker to move the piles from the yard to the area designed here for mulching.

Fabien's son, Chris is with us again for a while, and we have been having nightly movies. We watched "I can Only Imagine" which is the true account of the author Bart. He wrote this Song after his father died. Bart was abused as a child, and ended up leaving his Dad. He followed his dream with his band, but they hit a wall with their music, Bart was told by his music producer, "Find your 'heart'! Deal with whatever it is that was 'blocking you' from writing more compelling songs!" Bart sent his other band members off and went home to see his Dad. His Dad had been writing him letters, but Bart was so angry with his Dad that he never read not even one of his Dad's letters. But his Dad had been listening to his son. His Dad had turned to the Lord, and asked Jesus for forgiveness and to come into his heart. He Dad had pancreatic cancer. Bart ended up home just in time to help his father before he died. They were able to repair their relationship. Bart had gone to a Christian Camp when he was young and at that Camp, he was given a Journal, and told to write this,

"Lord, I ask you to help me to forgive _____. " and to fill in the blank space. As a child, he was not able to forgive his Father, so he left the space 'blank'. When he was with his father back home, he went to his room and found that Journal, and wrote in "DAD". At his father's funeral, one of his father's neighbor friends sat next to Bart, and nudged him and said, "Can you just imagine what he is seeing RIGHT NOW!" And that statement made Bart think again and again about his Dad who was now in heaven. As he went back to be with his band friends, while he was on the bus, he wrote the lyrics to, "I Can Only Imagine."

Bart says at the end of the documentary film that he went from hating his father who he saw as a literal 'monster' to seeing him as a loving father. He told the presidential congress in 2017 when he was asked to visit and give his testimony, "If Jesus Christ can change my monster father, into a loving father – God can do anything!"

I can only imagine - Can you imagine, just standing before the King

Ooooh I can only imagine What it would be like

When I walk, by your side -- I can only imagine, yeah

What my eyes would see, -- When your face, is before me

I can only imagine, I can only imagine -To be surrounded by your glory

What will my heart feel -- Will I dance for you Jesus

Or in awe of you be still --Will I stand in your presence

To my knees will I fall- Will I sing hallelujah - Will I be able to speak at all

I can only imagine, yeah, I can only imagine.

Chapter 11

Spiders and Bees: The November Letters

Be still, and know that I am God: I will be exalted among the heathen, I will be exalted in the earth.

Psalm 46:10

When I was a child there were spider webs that formed on the sides of the entry to the barns. The webs and the spiders were large and I was afraid to even go under their webs. Of course, spiders have a purpose beyond being scary! When we are afraid and still continue believe God, God is pleased! God has promised in Romans 8:28: "to work EVERYTHING together for 'good' to them that love God. "How' that happens is NOT in our hands. How God is able to make 'evil' become 'good' is a mystery. Jesus Christ is the biggest example of God turning 'bad' into 'good. He went about doing God's will, performing miracles, feeding thousands, healing the blind, restoring life to the man being carried out dead, to the young girl, and to Lazarus. The Pharisees were angry and concerned because he was healing on the Sabbath Day. In order to preserve their foundational faith, they determined Jesus must be dealt with. They had him arrested in the middle of the night, and then violated their own laws to condemn him. He was delivered to Pilate who declared, "I find no fault in Him!", who then sent him to Herod, who returned him to Pilate. Pilate, In an attempt to release him, had Jesus scourged with a whip with 39 lashes. The guards mocked him and placed a crown of thorns upon his head. Pilate washed his hands before the crowd that demanded he release Barabus and crucify Jesus. Jesus was nailed to a wooden cross and died and was buried in the rich man's tomb. But 3 days later, there was the empty tomb! Two angels sat upon the top of a rolled away stone declaring that He was alive, asking, "Why seek ye the living among the dead? He is not here, but has risen" (Luke 24:5-6). In 1 Corinthians 15: 1-11 the account is written that Jesus was seen by over 500 people at one time before he ascended bodily in a cloud into heaven. Then, as those people stood and watched, two men came down from heaven and gave the great commission to 'Go the whole world over and proclaim the good news to all mankind" (Mark 16:15). The fulfillment of God's "peace on earth" will come when Jesus Christ returns to set up His Kingdom on earth. Until then we are told to be like the 'Bees' – busy about His work!

BEES for Believers

BE KIND: And be ye kind one to another, tenderhearted, forgiving one another, even as God for Christ's sake hath forgiven you" (Ephesians 6:32).

BE THANKFUL: "Enter into his gates with thanksgiving and into his courts with praise, be thankful unto him and bless his name" (Psalm 100:4).

BE DOERS: "But be ye doers of the word, and not hearers only, deceiving your own selves" (James 1:22).

BE MERCIFUL: "Be ye therefore merciful as your Father also is merciful" (Luke 6:36).

BE READY TO GIVE AN ANSWER: "But sanctify the Lord God in your hearts: and be ready always to give an answer to every man that asketh you a reason of the hope that is in you with meekness and fear" (1 Peter

3:15).

BE STRONG: "Finally, my brethren, be strong in the Lord, and in the power of his might" (Ephesians 6:10).

BE FRUITFUL: "That ye might walk worthy of the Lord unto all pleasing, being fruitful in every good work, and increasing in the knowledge of God" (Colossians 1:10).

BE TRANSFORMED: "And be not confirmed to this world: but be ye transformed by the renewing of your mind, that ye may prove what is that good, and acceptable, and perfect, will of God" (Romans 12:2).

BE AN EXAMPLE: Let no man despise thy youth: but he thou an example of the believers, in word, in conversation, in charity, in spirit, in faith, in purity" (1 Timothy 4:12).

BE HOLY: "But as he which hath called you is holy, so be ye holy in all manner of conversations" (1 Peter 1:15).

BE STEADFAST: "Wherefore, my beloved brethren, be ye steadfast, unmovable, always abounding in the work of the Lord, forasmuch as ye know that your labor is not in vain in the Lord" (1 Corinthians 15:58).

BE READY: "Therefore be ye also ready: for in such an hour as ye think not the Son of man cometh" (Matthew 24:14).

THE NOVEMBER LETTERS

November 6, 2020 Dear (Name)

We have had our first snow fall, about 2 inches, followed by another 3 inches overnight. That, today, has all now melted. There is still a lot of work left to do on leaf pickup so we are glad that we have a small window to do what remains. But Grady had his first opportunity to experience snow. At first, he was afraid, but a moment later he was jumping and playing in the piles of snow. Very entertaining to watch. He never ceases to find ways to entertain himself!

Our Presidential election, at the moment, appears to be going to Biden. My concerns center around religious freedom, of more abortions, as well as a socialist implementation of a one world government, one world monetary system, and one world religion that includes allowances for just about everything except for those who actually believe in the words of the Lord Jesus Christ and who rose from the dead, which is something that no other person in history has ever done!

"For there is none other name under heaven given among men, whereby we must be saved." Acts 4:12.

Listening to the news anchors who are rejoicing that they will no longer have anything to report without Donald Trump to bash and condemn is very telling in and of itself. We do live in trying times.

My left hip has slipped out of its socket, which is very painful. I have been to the chiropractor and that has helped, but am now very sore from having the adjustment done. It will take about 3 days for the soreness to wear off. So, my daily agenda has slowed to a crawl. I get up in the morning and have my Bible time and prayer time, and then get into clearing out the work that needs to be done on the three Journals. Fortunately, I am quite caught up. I have been able to maintain my work in the midst of my physical pain. I have a heating pad on my hip area and that seems to help a lot. I also have been sleeping with a heated rice bag, and have reverted to sleeping on the floor. That seems to be the only place that I can actually be comfortable enough to sleep. Fabien has gotten up out of bed to bring me heated rice bags because it is a challenge for me to get up once I am down. I am encouraged that in about 3 days I will be much better. For now, I am experiencing first hand. Romans 8:18: **For I reckon that the sufferings of this present time are not worthy to be compared with the glory which shall be revealed in us.**

November 13, 2020 Dear (Name)

Am back to normal and feeling better. I am being careful not to lift anything too heavy and I am back to doing my daily exercise stretches and walking routine.

There are COVID restrictions again in place in Vermont and we are being asked to NOT gather for Thanksgiving or in groups of more than 10 in an attempt to prevent more spikes from occurring.

Also, things with the election are still up in the air. There really isn't much that anyone can do to change things. I told my friends at UVM when I was asked what I thought about all of it and what was I doing, that I was 'praying'. My friend Marti asked, "Praying." I replied, "Yes, praying that we don't have someone killed before this is over." She had not thought of praying about it at all!

Chris finally has the furnace hooked up at his home in Richford and heat is coming out their house registers. Bobbie is very happy to be able to have a warm house and to be able to sleep in a warm place. Adam Taft's outdoor stair project to create a stairway to connect the 2nd story to the ground is almost finished. We have had incredible weather here. I have been able to wear my summer dresses outside 3 days in a row. We had a high of 70 in Highgate on Nov. 10. Fabien has been able to get the gutters cleaned out and to install some leave guards in both the front and back high gutter areas of our home. This will be a BIG help to keep the gutters working and to keep them from getting clogged up.

Chris and Bobby both came to church on Sunday. The message was that we are not alone through difficulties. God leads us all along the way. We are called by 'name' Isaiah 43:1-3 and told to" Fear not!" In life, we are asked to go through our own seasons of storms, wind, snow, as well as heat and drought. These TEST our faith but God has promised to get us through I. Our steps are ordered by the Lord Psalm 37:23. Our role is to Love God and one another, and be faithful in the small things, following the Lord, faithfully praying about all things.

One of the promises made early in Jesus's ministry was to Nathaniel. He was told, "Hereafter ye shall see heaven open and the angels of God, ascending and descending upon the Son of Man." John 1:51 --such an amazing promise, and I do not believe this promise has had its fulfillment yet on earth. In truth, we belong to God for all eternity. Each day we have the opportunity to do 'holy labor' and to be doubly diligent in His business, always prepared to be able to give an answer to those we meet of the assurance of eternal life through Jesus's work on the cross. Our part is to 'strive for victory' in all things. Charles Spurgeon wrote, "Spices are most fragrant when burnt and bruised." When we venture out to sow the Word of God in the hearts of those we meet, we are in truth gifting them a divine product that everyone is truly desirous to have: **Faith, patience, endurance and steadfastness.** It all starts with FAITH. "And Faith cometh by hearing and hearing by the Word of God" (Romans 10:17.)

"Without FAITH it is impossible to please God for he that comes to God, must believe that He is and that He is a rewarder of those who **DILIGENTLY** seek Him" (Hebrews 11:6). The God we serve is **GREAT!** **Abba** -Our Father/ **Ancient of Days** -existing eternally/ **El-Roi** – God who sees/ **El Shaddai** – God Almighty**/ Emanuel** God with us/ **Elohim** -The Creator! *We CANNOT be apart from HIM at any time – because 'in Him, we live and move and have our being".*

November 16, 2020 Hi (Name)

The most important part of life is indeed 'character' and 'truth' and living life without compromise. Fabien and I watched the account of Joseph in the Bible this week. The commentary spoke of how each unjust event tried his character, and provided him with the opportunity to grow in grace in spite of the evil that was done to him. He never lost his faith in God, or his desire to live his life to please and honor God above all else.

Vermont is back under restrictions related to COVID, and we are working to remain home and to avoid having to go places as much as possible.

It is just living one day at a time, and being grateful for the things that we do have each day, and praying for the Lord to provide a way for us to be able to have 'victory' through these trials of our faith.

Chris spent the weekend in Richford but is back today for the week. My greatest prayer is that he will continue to 'move forward' and not turn back to running away from issues by numbing himself with alcohol. This is a hard pattern for him to break, but if he does not have victory over it, it surely will likely continue to destroy his relationship with his family, as it places that above everything else, and the cost is something that he does not factor in -believing all will continue to be 'okay' and that there are no 'real consequences' to his choices. Our Lord is able to turn all of us around to wanting to seek Him above all else.

November 25, 2020 Dear (Name),
Our church had an evening Thanksgiving Service last night. The Pastor opened the service for people to share experiences for which they were 'thankful'. People shared pieces of their life that on the surface appeared to NOT be anything to be grateful for at all. One man had been without a job for many months and yet he was thankful for the Lord had provided for his family in unusual ways.

Another woman's life was one challenge after another, yet in the middle of all of the 'mess' she was thankful to the Lord because she had not lost faith in the midst of the trials. There is actually nowhere in the Bible that believers are promised an 'easy' road, rather the Lord has promised to provide a 'way THROUGH life's challenges and for that we can truly be THANKFUL!

True believers who look to Jesus Christ for their salvation receive God's Holy Spirit who enables our FAITH to OVERCOME our fears and that gives us a truly thankful heart in the midst of life's 'trouble and wow'. God uses trials to change us from 'rough diamonds' into 'priceless gems that reflect His likeness when we exhibit the fruit of His Holy Spirit: His love, joy, peace, longsuffering, patience, goodness, faith, temperance and self-control.

The tests of life will produce within us sometimes 'laughter', sometime 'tears'. The Lord collects all of our tears and will return them someday to us when we get to heaven for special rewards. Remember: The Lord has promised to work 'it' all for our good. Sometimes I talk out loud and say, "Okay! Lord, I am going to WAIT for you to WORK THIS for good!" Then, I literally 'let it go'. Or I tell the Lord, "I am GIVING this to you! There is NOTHING I can do here to change anything but I am GIVING it to you –

You do the work that needs to be done here!" Both produce within me a 'release' and a level of 'peace that passes my ability to understand. This is how FAITH is able to lift burdens into another dimension and help us to move on. God provides 'the way'. Our work is to yield and follow Him. The Lord is the 'potter' – we are the 'clay'.

God is able to take lemons and make them into lemonade. When we do this, it is well pleasing in God's sight. We were created to give God our thanks and praise. It is work to be an overcomer and to LOOK for ways to thank the Lord, to PRAY about things that bother us. And when we do these things, the door is opened for us to PRAISE the Lord for hearing our prayers.

The Lord is VERY aware of what is going on. Jesus told the disciples to let the 'tares' grow with the 'wheat' until the harvest. There is a time in the future when the Lord will reconcile all things unto Himself.

When life makes us feel like we have been tossed into dryer, just tossed up/down/and all around we must exercise FAITH in God. Prayer 'turns off' the spin cycle. So, take COURAGE, have FAITH, and PRAY! Ask God for help – God is ABLE to do abundantly above all that we ask or think, and the Lord has promised to hear and answer our prayers. We are told to PRAY and WAIT. I am thankful to God who has promised to never leave us nor forsake us! He is a friend that sticketh closer than a brother. Proverbs 18:24.

"Blessed be God, even the Father of our Lord Jesus Christ, the Father of mercies, and the God of all comfort; Who comforteth us in all our tribulation, that we may be able to comfort them which are in any trouble, by the comfort wherewith we ourselves are comforted of God" (2 Corinthians 3:1-6).

"The Lord knoweth how to deliver the godly out of temptations, and to reserve the unjust unto the day of judgment to be punished" (2 Peter 2:9).

Chapter 12

The Choice: The December Letters

Bless the Lord, O my soul, and forget not all His Benefits.

Psalm 103:2

It is always easier to see the purpose of life when you look backwards from a life lived. There is no way for us to see around a 'corner' without actually going around the corner. It was going around a corner when I was just 5 years old that would impact my entire life.

One of the things I loved to do as a child, was to take my doll in her baby carriage and push her around our very long driveway. But my sisters did not appreciate my dolls, and threatened to take them and throw them on the ground. That scared me, so I worked to not let that happen. That meant that when I took my baby carriage out, I would only use it on the lower section of the driveway. I refused to go around the corner because I knew that meant my doll could be taken from me. But, one day I became bored, and determined to go around that corner. I would fight to keep my doll safe! So, although very scared, I pushed my baby carriage right around that corner! When I got around the corner, I stopped and looked. No one was there! No one! I was all alone, and I was truly very happy. But I was also confused. Then I heard a voice say to me, "Play with your dolls, Dawn, you will not always be able to play with your dolls!" So, play I did! That experience remained with me as a 'pivotal moment in time'. When I was older, and challenges arrived, and I was afraid, I would remember that 'corner'. And even now, when there seems to be 'no way' and 'no hope' I know that God can provide a way of escape!

I am encouraged by the example of the Lord Jesus Christ's walk of faith. He spent a lot of time in prayer. He began by rising early and praying. Sometimes he prayed all night.

We have a CHOICE! Move forward in FAITH, believing that we have an advocate in Heaven or walk in fear. God did in fact raise Jesus from the grave (Mark 16:42). Angels appeared and proclaimed, "He is not here: for He is risen as he said" (Matthew 28:6).

"I would have you WISE unto that which is good (prayer, fasting, consecration, separation, worship, praise, thanksgiving, service, sacrifice) and SIMPLE concerning evil" (Romans 16:19).

We are to look 'past' evil, we are not be overcome by evil. We are not to be like the Pharisees' and be hung up on 'outward appearance'. This is in effect putting a 'cart' before a 'horse'. The horse must be in front of the cart to pull the cart. God views the 'heart'. God works from the 'inside out'. The work of God is a 'heart' thing; it is not a 'head' understanding thing. It does not matter what "I" or 'anyone' else 'thinks'. What matters is what God says.

How does this work?

"GRACE (God's undeserved MERCY) and PEACE (knowing God is in control no matter what we see) BE MULTIPLED (become applied to every area of our life, in every situation, every moment of time) **through the knowledge of GOD that ye might be partakers of the DIVINE NATURE"** (1 Peter 1:3).

What will this do?

We will have 'escaped the corruption that is in the world through lust" (1 Peter 1:4).

How will that occur?

Think of 8 stepping stones or stairs that go upward. Steps that begin with the act of simple FAITH in God and his Son Jesus Christ (1 Peter 1:4).

Step 1: Apply FAITH by asking Him, "Lord, I believe, have mercy on me!"

Step 2: Give 'all diligence' to add to your Faith: VIRTUE (honesty)

Step 3: And to Virtue: KNOWLEDGE (Read the Bible)

Step 4: And to Knowledge: TEMPERANCE (Apply lessons to your life)

Step 5: And to Temperance: PATIENCE (Be willing to wait for God)

Step 6: And to Patience: GODLINESS (Have attitude of gratitude)

Step 7: And to Godliness: BROTHERLY KINDNESS (Share what you have)

Step 8: and to Brotherly Kindness: CHARITY (LOVE) (Focus on God and others above yourself).

"When" do we do these things?

Day and night: "mediate on it day and night" (Joshua 1:8). No matter what you 'see' know that God is in control and has a purpose.

"Ye are enriched (gaining ground) by Him in all utterance (things said) and in all knowledge (things presented)" (1 Corinthians 1:5).

Charles Spurgeon said it best: "We find no rest unless we turn to Him. We are driven to Jesus by an unrest which finds no remedy elsewhere. At Christ's command, it is WISE to let down the net at the very spot where we have toiled in vain all night."

Thomas Manton said:

"A sundial, if the sun shines not, we cannot tell the time of day."

"Enter His GATES with THANKSGIVING and His Courts with PRAISE" (Psalm 100:4).

"Say among the heathen that the Lord reigneth" (Psalm 96:10).

"Honor and Majesty are before Him. Strength and beauty are in His sanctuary" (Psalm 96:6).

"For the Lord is a great God and a Great King above all gods" (Psalm 100:2).

"Because he hath set his LOVE upon me therefore I will deliver him; I will set him on high because he hath known my name. He shall call upon me and I will answer him. I will be with him in TROUBLE, I will DELIVER him, and honor him with long life will I satisfy him and shew him my salvation" (Psalm 91:14).

"I will say of the Lord He is my refuge and my fortress, my God in Hi will I trust" (Psalm 91:1).

"The sacrifice of God are a broken spirit and a broken and contrite heart, O Lord thou wilt not despise" (Psalm 51:17).

THE DECEMBER LETTERS

December 4, 2020   Dear (Name)

My sister's beloved Cricket Yorkie had to be put 'down' I got to say my goodbye to her. Treya and Ron then arranged for her to have a shot to put her to sleep. She was truly a 'pain in the backside' but we are missing our little determined dog who could run faster than all of us.

Joyce Meyer has a new book, 'Do it Afraid'. Most of us can be frozen by fear: fear of what people will think of us, fear of rejection, fear of failure, fear of success. We are told to not FEAR: i.e. 'Fear not. "and that is because there are things that cause great fear inside of us. We must go forward" anyway. Singing a song when we are the most afraid, will empower us to get us through that particular challenge. Fabien and I talked about our own lives. Fear causes our mind to go to the worst possible scenario and then we can fill in the blanks with a lot of 'What if's". Faith does the exact opposite. FAITH looks BEYOND the problem and to the Lord and then we can PRAY. The truth is "no one knows the future". God is unlimited in what he can do!"

Our Northside message was on the Simplicity of the true meaning of Christmas. God sent the angel Gabriel to Mary. "And the angel said unto her, Fear not, Mary: for thou hast found favor with God And, behold, thou shalt conceive in thy womb, and bring forth a son, and shalt call his name JESUS. He shall be great, and shall be called the Son of the Highest: and the Lord God shall give unto him the throne of his father David: And he shall reign over the house of Jacob for ever; and <u>of his kingdom there shall be no end</u>. Luke 2:30-33.

This is so amazing. The mission of the Angel Gabriel warms my heart. This angelic message compels me to share it with everyone! Read it again! What HOPE! Mary and Joseph 'did it afraid!' - they TRUSTED God day by day.

We HAVE assurance of ETERNAL LIFE – because God LOVED us SO MUCH that He actually came down to dwell with us, through the Son of God – JESUS. His perfect life of obedience to God even to the dying on a cross, was honored by God RAISING HIM from the DEAD! He is ALIVE FOREVER more! I am like the thief who cried out "Remember me when I come into your Kingdom!" Jesus replied, 'Today! They shalt be with me in paradise. Let us also cry out so that on a day to come we too will hear Jesus say to us "Welcome to paradise!"

For now, we are His sheep: "The sheep hear His voice and <u>He calleth his own sheep by name</u> and leadeth them out. He goeth before them and the sheep follow Him for, <u>they KNOW HIS VOICE</u>" (John 10:3-4).

December 10, 2020 Dear (Name),

The good news is that Chris has past his 45th day and is working to make 60 days. He says he cannot use the word "fine" anymore because that is what he used to tell everyone, "I'm fine!" but he was 'not fine'. He told us he is struggling but is 'okay'. I told him the Lord had showed me how incredible eternity will be, and that between now and THEN - each day is our 'opportunity' to 'redeem' the time. When I realized this, it was as though a 'barrier' within my heart 'let go' to allow a new desire to rush in to work to do my very best in whatever I am asked to do. Much of the 'work of life' is 'routine' and can be done without my whole heart joining into the activity. The work gets done, but is done without much enthusiasm. Knowing the Lord is actually pleased when we 'rise' and commit to doing our very best – is a motivator for my soul. When we are yielded, to God he provides us with His Holy Spirit's empowerment for the task. This awareness is 'fuel' to my soul. "Offer unto God THANKSGIVING and pay thy vows unto the most High and CALL upon me in the day of trouble. I will deliver thee and thou shalt glorify me" (Psalm 50:14&15).

My retired friends asked me join them in identifying favorite songs. I really did not want to play the 'Song game' but I asked the Lord to help me to play the game. The request was to identify a song that makes you 'happy'. My pick was 'The Drummer Boy" which is the pa rum pa pum song. One of the picks from my friend Mary was "Wanting Memories" by Reh Roshel. The lyrics at the end are that memories allow us to see things from another's eyes. I was asked why I had picked my song, "The Drummer Boy". I told them that it my song was linked to Mary's Memories song. In fact, Mary was involved with an event that I had oversight for at UVM, that had a very complex set up and take down. One year was particularly challenging. At the end of that event, I went to KFC for dinner before heading to my caregiving overnight assignment. At KFC I got my order and sat down to eat. Once seated, the song the Drummer Boy started to play. One by one people in the restaurant began to sing. Soon we all were singing together instead of eating. When the song finished, I told the Lord that my UVM Event was 'my drum' and that I had truly 'done by very best' for Him that day. I finished my meal and headed out the door, only to meet a very young couple coming in with a brand-new baby in a baby carrier. I told them that it was wonderful they had a new child for the Christmas season, and just as the words came out of my mouth, the baby in the carrier, turned its head and looked straight at me and smiled at me! The couple had no idea we had just been singing The Drummer Boy. The last lyric of the song is, " and then He smiled at me. Pa rum pa pa pum, me and my drum." For me it was a Divine confirmation that my 'gift' of working on the event was 'received' just as was the boy's playing on his drum. This brings joy unspeakable when we KNOW that God IS PLEASED with us. When we suffer, and do not lose faith, this pleases God!

We must be like Mary and Joseph and act upon what is given to us. uture. The wise men went in HOPE. The Shepherds got up and WENT to see. We are to HOPE in GOD, to walk in FAITH not by sight. Herod, went by **SIGHT**; knowing the wise men went back another way, he ordered all of the children under 2 to be killed in Bethlehem to ensure he remained King. God allows 'bad' to happen. For now, the 'weeds and tares' grow with the 'wheat'. But a time is coming when this will no longer be allowed. God has promised to make all things right. **This is HOPE!**

December 16, 2020 Dear (Name)

We are having below zero temperatures here for the first time this year. Grady and the other cats are being kept inside by my sister Audrey – it is too cold for them to be outside for very long. Grady was not very happy this morning. Audrey warned me he was headed to my stairs to come up in order to go outside. Usually, he comes to the back French door and 'meows to come 'in'. Almost immediately Grady was meowing at our inner door. I went and opened the door and got him to play with a toy, but that didn't last long. I decided to put on my coat and hat and take him to our garage. Once inside our garage he was investigating that space. Then I took him back inside and returned him to Audrey downstairs, somewhat tired and wore out from his latest adventure.

Our friend from Enosburg texted about a skunk she named Chanel. She wrote, "What brought joy to my heart, mind and soul at around midnight, was watching "Chanel' the large elegant skunk peacefully eating the peanut butter sandwiches at the Critter Diner that I put out." I called her and she told me she is feeding squirrels and racoons too, and she was really enjoying seeing them come and dine.

My Dad used to love to see the birds come to a bird feeder, and to see raccoons come to knock that bird feeder onto the ground to get the birdseed. One of my joys is seeing a bird come to the back deck when I am working on my laptop. Certainly, the Lord has created a very diverse world that proclaims His glory.

God's simple Peace is really what we all desire. It is actually 'peace' that is NOT from things going our way. God's peace comes to those who submit their life to God and to His Will for their life. It is a Peace that comes from a real 'relationship' with God through His Holy Spirit given to us through Jesus Christ. God needs to be at the Center of all we do because that is what lines us up to be willing to be under God's authority. The world, as beautiful as it is, full of 'things' to see and 'things' to do, will always make us 'hungry' for MORE. Nothing here can satisfy the inner spiritual hole that is within us. As long as we choose to chase "worldly things" we will be ever searching for more. Like Grady, we will continue to 'wear ourselves out" only to get up and do it again and again. This is like a dog chasing its tail, once we have what we 'think' we want, we find that it is not ABLE to satisfy our inner longing. What can possibly make us stop? Well, it is the hard times that make us 'stop' and consider. When things are going 'wrong,' that is when we are open to ask God for His help. God created us to have fellowship with Him. The difficult times make us ask,' Why?" The account of 'Job' in the Bible tells that he lost everything overnight. He exclaimed, "The Lord giveth and the Lord taketh away – blessed be the name of the Lord." His experience made him long to understand. So, he prayed and sought God. Once connected with God he had 'peace' in spite of his circumstances. Job had to wait for God's timing, but God restored Job's life. And God will restore us as well, and get us through trials in ways we do not expect when with our 'heart' we, too, call upon His Name!

Romans 5:1: "Therefore being justified by faith, we have peace with God through our Lord Jesus Christ".

Isaiah 9:6: "For unto us a child is born, unto us a son is given: and the government shall be upon his shoulder: and his name shall be called Wonderful, Counsellor, The mighty God, The everlasting Father, The Prince of Peace."

The Jews were looking for 'political peace' – but that will not come until Jesus Christ returns to earth. What Jesus came to bring was 'Restoration' between man and God – Jesus paid for our sins, and God accepted His sacrificial life as payment in full. This is the greatest of all 'gifts' from God to men.

"The Lord hath done great things for us and whereof we are glad" (Psalm 126:3)

December 23, 2020 Dear (Name)

It seems 'Chanel' the elegant skunk has showed-off her skills. After my friend had placed her menu out in the 'Critter Diner', a possum and two skunks wandered right in. Chanel, at the sight of a second skunk, stomped her feet, lifted her tail, and released her cocktail into the air. The possum immediately collapsed to the ground and played 'dead". The second skunk got a lethal dose and ran full speed down the street. The smell lingered into the next day. My friend saw the entire episode and felt it was worth the inconvenience. She did move her Critter diner though, and placed a sign, "Manners required here!"

Chris and Fabien have been making Children's play gyms. It actually looks like a 'wooden clothes rack' that folds up. The dowels are large ones for small hands and feet to climb up so they can go then slide down. Chris is continuing to stay the course. We are truly praying he will continue moving forward for his life and marriage.

We got snow that may last for Christmas. We missed the big storm. But my sister in Rutland got 2 feet of snow. Our home farm received 3 inches, Burlington got 5 inches.

Northside Church will hold a candlelight service Christmas Eve. The message this Sunday was on the Joy that comes from our Creator. Life provides us with experiences that can give us God's 'joy'. It is our circumstances that threaten to 'rob us of that joy'.

The woman that Jesus met at the well, was getting her water at high noon, the hottest time of the day to enable her to AVOID meeting people that would criticize her. When the Lord offered her 'living water' she willing asked for that 'water' so she would 'thirst' no more! Jesus asked her to call her husband. She responded that she had no husband. Jesus acknowledged she had no husband, and had actually been with five men, and the one she was with 'now' was not her husband. The point Jesus made to her was that her actions were unable to brin her joy because she was focused just on 'herself'. We, too, can look for satisfaction apart from 'fellowship' with God. We can work to 'fill up' our life with what we 'think' will make us happy, but our real need is, also, for fellowship with God and His Holy Spirit, and with others.

Isaiah 9:6 describes God:

Wonderful -filled with 'wonder'

Counselor – 'come! For help to navigate through life;

The Everlasting Father – constantly available to us

The Prince of Peace – who offers a different view of 'life' which removes stress, anxiety, worry, and fear.

Jesus came to DIE for sins – yours and mine. When we ask Him to forgive us, He does! His promises in the Bible, bring AWE and that Awe causes us to desire more of Him.

Romans 5:1 explains Jesus agreed to suffer because it would provide salvation for all who believe and ask. It is Jesus that offers assurance that though we 'die' yet shall we live – because He conquered death and is ALIVE Forever more. Receiving God's unconditional love, forgiveness, and mercy for us, is what GIVES us His assurance of salvation – and that is the REAL Joy of Christmas!

December 30, 2020 Dear (Name)

We had a very low-key Christmas here. We took in our respite person Dave. Because he was with us on Christmas Day, Fabien and I agreed we needed to get him a couple of presents, and, that if we gave him presents, that would mean we, too, would have to have a couple presents, so we could have an official 'present exchange'. We got him a bag of his favorite Smart Food popcorn, and a case of ginger ale. When he arrived, he handed me a present of 'Smartfood popcorn' for Fabien. I quickly put it into a paper bag and placed it in front of our 'fireplace'. Once we all settled in, I handed Dave our wrapped gift and Fabien's Dave's gift. I said, 'These gifts need to be opened 'together'. They both opened their gift – and SMILED and looked at each other as they held their bags in the air! Dave giggled, "We each got the same thing!" It was a precious moment for sure.

My sister Audrey has chickens and our neighbor Virginia has turkeys, roosters and chickens which come to Audrey's coup area typically every day to eat what Audrey places on the ground for them. Her 'feeding ground area' needs to be 'scrapped' every few months to keep the area from becoming very slippery. Audrey told me she it really needed to be cleaned up and she was planning on doing the hoeing herself. Christmas day was 60 degrees here! Fabien and I sat and talked outside on his garage with just shirts on, no coats needed! As we visited, he pointed to our outdoor bench that the wind knocked over. He said, "Likely it's broken as I can see it looks like it hit the tree behind it." We got up to walk down to check out the bench and as we walked, I mentioned we needed to help Audrey scrapping down the front coup ground area. Fabien turned and we headed now for that area to go and take a peek at how bad it was. Fabien grabbed the hoe and started to scrap the ground. I watched as he made several piles. Then, he went and got his tractor with its bucket and came and used the tractor to scrap the entire area, and then pick up the piles we created. I helped with the hoeing and kept the end trails from his tractor shovel cleaned up. The entire area looked incredibly wonderful when he was done. No more 'tracking in' chicken poop into the entry of Audrey's. While he worked, I created a short phone video of Fabien doing the work, and then sent that to Audrey to wish her a Merry Christmas with the video.

Our church message was on real surrender being a 'moment by moment' adventure with an 'eternal' focus aimed at pleasing God more than ourselves. Truly we were created to be tools and vessels for His use. When we walk with His Holy Spirit, there is newness of life, as He convicts us to give up being a 'slave' to our own fleshly desires. It is our repentance that opens a door of empowerment for us to 'walk with God'. There is no 'loss' with surrender -- for we gain far more than we ever loose. God's business is 'mending' our brokenness. We are enabled to 'gift' our 'life' back to God. Most Christians believe in 'piece-meal' surrender – i.e., just a little at a time. When we purchase a car, we get the entire car all at once We would be shocked if a dealer came out to us with boxes filled with car parts. Without the entire car, we cannot go anywhere. It is our total surrender to the Lord, that opens the doors to His abundant life. Our own wants and desires keep us chained and anchored to 'what we think' is good. Our entire purpose is to GIVE ourselves to God. When we do THAT, God is able to then use us to show His mercy to others. We are Christ's hands, and feet, eyes and ears, and mouth. There is DIVINE power in obedience to His leading. And the best part of all, is:

"And we know that all things work together for good to them that love God, to them who are the called according to his purpose" (Romans 8:28).

Below is a letter I received from an inmate:

December 15, 2020

Dear Dawn,

I must tell you that your letters have brought many smiles and much joy to me. And I thank God and you for them. Sorry about not writing; just never much for writing and expressing my thoughts and feelings. But a giant 'Thank You' - you will never know how your letters have helped in many ways.

May Our Lord and God, bless you and all of yours. Praying His Great and Glorious Will be done in the days ahead in all our live.

Thank you,

Terry

And here is my letter back to Terry:

December 28, 2020

Hi Terry,

Thank you so very much for your card and note.

Just about the date you wrote your note, I had prayed that the Lord would let me know from someone if the letters were even worth sending. Your letting me know that they deliver some joy meant a lot to me.

Your card was quite powerful because it was of a sleigh with horses with a lot of people in the sled.

I actually have a music box with the same image but there are only 2 people in the sled with one horse. It was a reminder to me that the Lord is working to ensure that His House is Full of the Praise that is due his Holy name and that His Word will NOT return void.

We can indeed 'join ourselves to the Lord's Holy Spirit' and then like those horses, He will daily 'pull' us along where He wants us to go, guiding our thoughts and actions as we go.

My understanding of the role of God's Holy Spirit in my life continues to evolve in a greater way, which delivers much peace to the moments of each day.

Ironically, each week that comes I have no idea what I am going to say in my letter. I have to pray and just ask the Lord to help me to write something that is more than, I cleaned the house and did my online Journals.

Today, 'Grady' came upstairs and joined me next to my computer and then decided it was a good idea to jump up and see what was holding my attention, even walking on my keyboard. He has gotten to be quite a BIG cat! Audrey told me he brought in a mole and placed it on her carpet and when she went to pick it up, he quickly swallowed the entire thing! She was amazed to see it happen so quick.

I continue to pray for you and others for strength, courage, and peace in the midst of the 'trial' of being in a place that is not 'home' having to deal with things I am sure you would be just thrilled to be away from.

Know that you are not forgotten and that the Lord's love is with you at all times.

Best

Dawn

You may go to Heaven:

Without **health**,

Without **wealth**;

Without **fame**,

Without a **great name**;

Without **learning**,

Without **earnings**;

Without **culture**,

Without **beauty**;

Without **friends**,

Without ten thousand other things . . .

BUT you can't go to Heaven WITHOUT CHRIST.

"Neither is there salvation in any other: for there is none other name under heaven given among men, WHEREBY WE MUST BE SAVED" (Acts 4:12)

(Read: John 3, Romans 3, Ephesians 2)

FROM: SOWERS OF SEED, INC, P.O. Box 6217, Ft. Worth, TX 76115

Bible Promises of the Return of Jesus Christ to Earth:

This same Jesus, which is taken up from you into heaven, shall so come in like manner as ye have seen him go into heaven. Acts 1:11

For the Lord himself shall descend from heaven with a shout, with the voice of the archangel, and with the trump of God: and the dead in Christ shall rise first: Then we which are alive and remain shall be caught up together with them in the clouds, to meet the Lord in the air: and so shall we ever be with the lord.

1 Thessalonians 4:16-17

The Disciples ask: Tell us, when shall these things be? And what shall be the sign of thy coming, and of the end of the world?

And Jesus answered and said unto them, Take heed that no man deceive you. For many shall come in my name, saying, I am Christ; and shall deceive many.

And ye shall hear of wars and rumors of wars: see that ye be not troubled: for all these things must come to pass, but the end is not yet.

For nation shall rise against nation, and kingdom against kingdom, and there shall be famines, and pestilences, and earthquakes, in divers' places. All these are the beginning of sorrows. Then shall they deliver you up to be afflicted, and shall kill you: and ye shall be hated of all nations for my name's sake.

And then shall many be offended, and shall betray one another, and shall hate one another. And many false prophets shall rise, and shall deceive many. And because iniquity shall abound, the love of many shall wax cold. Matthew 24: 3-12

And this gospel of the kingdom shall be preached in all the world for a witness unto all nations; and then shall the end come. Matthew 24:14

For then shall be great tribulation, such as was not since the beginning of the world to this time, no, nor ever shall be. And <u>except those days should be shortened</u>, there should no flesh be saved; but for the elect's sake <u>those days shall be shortened</u>. Then if any man shall say unto you. Lo, here is Christ, or there; believe it not. For there shall arise false Christs, and false prophets, and shall shew great signs and wonders; insomuch that, if it were possible, they shall deceive the very elect. Behold, I have told you before. Wherefore if they shall say unto you, Behold, he is in the desert; go not forth: behold he is in the secret chambers; believe it not.

For as the lightning cometh out of the east, and shineth even unto the west; so, shall also the coming of the Son of man be. Matthew 24:21-27

But of that day and hour knoweth no man, no, not the angels of heaven, but my Father only.

But as the days of Noah were, so shall also the coming of the Son of man be. For as in the days that were before the flood they were eating and drinking, marrying and giving in marriage, until the day that Noe entered into the ark, and knew not until the flood came, and took them all away; so, shall also the coming of the son of man be. Matthew 24: 36-39

Watch therefore: for ye know not what hour your Lord doth come. Therefore, be ye also ready; for in such an hour as ye think not the son of man cometh. Matthew 24:42, 44

Denying ungodliness and worldly lusts, we should live soberly, righteously, and godly, in this present world; Looking for the blessed hope, and the glorious appearing of the great God and our Savior Jesus Christ. Timothy 2:12-13

Are you ready to meet Christ should He come today? You can be, if you are willing to accept Jesus Christ as your personal Savior.

The Provision of God: Salvation in Christ

But God commendeth his love toward us, in that, while we were yet sinners, Christ died for us. Romans 5:8

Who his own self bare our sins in his own body on the tree, that we, being dead to sins, should live unto righteousness: by whose stripes ye were healed. 1 Peter 2:24

He that believeth on the Son hath everlasting life; and he that believeth not the Son shall not see life; but the wrath of God abideth on him. John 3:36

Jesus saith unto him, I am the Way, the Truth, and the Life: no man cometh unto the Father, but by Me. John 14:6

Nether is there salvation in any other, for there is no other name unto heaven given among men, whereby we must be saved. Acts 4:12

. and the blood of Jesus Christ His Son cleanseth us from all sin. 1 John 1:7

The Prayer of Confession

That if thou shalt confess with thy mouth to the Lord Jesus, and shalt believe in thine heart that God hath raised Him from the dead, thou shalt be saved. For with the heart man believeth unto righteousness, and with the mouth confession is made unto salvation. Romans 10:9-10

Whosoever therefore shall confess me before men, him will I confess also before my Father which is in heaven. Matthew 10:32

MY PRAYER

"Lord Jesus, I am sorry for my sins, and I ask You to forgive me. I open the door of my heart, and receive You as my Lord and Savior. Take control of my life, and begin making me the person You want me to be. Thank you, Lord Jesus, for saving me and for hearing my prayer in Jesus' name. Amen"

The Power Available for the Christian Life

But ye shall receive power, after that the Holy Ghost is come upon you and ye shall be witnesses unto Me, both in Jerusalem, and in all Judea, and in Samaria, and unto the uttermost part of the earth. Acts 1:8

This I say then, walk in the Spirit, and ye shall not fulfil the lust of the flesh. Galatians 5:16

For God hath not given us the spirit of fear, but of power, and of love, and of a sound mind. 2 Timothy 1:7

But as it is written, eye hath not seen, nor ear heard, neither have entered into the heart of man, the things which God hath prepared for them that love Him. But God hath revealed them unto us by his

Spirit; for the Spirit searcheth all things, yea, the deep things of God. 1 Corinthians 2:9-10

These things I have spoken unto you, that in Me ye might have peace. In the world ye shall have tribulation; but be of good cheer; I have overcome the world. John 16:33

King of Kings, Lord of Lords, Shepherd, and Bishop of our souls. 1Tmothy 6:15

The Royal High Priest, redeeming by His blood multitudes of every tribe, tongue, people, and nation. 1 Peter 2:9 Rev. 5:9

Head of the Church. Ephesians 1:22

Elect of God; power and authority are His. Matthew 28:18

Let Jesus be King of your life
Read your Bible every day to get to know Christ better.
Talk to God in prayer every day.
Find a church where the Bible is taught as the complete Word of God, and is the final authority.

RESOURCE:

Radio Bible Class (RBC) Ministries is a great resource for understandable and accessible information about Jesus Christ and His Holy Bible. They offer online guidance and a free monthly devotional entitled, *"Our Daily Bread"* that contains encouragement, comfort, and His divine guidance. To learn more on how to be ready for His return, visit: http://rbc.org/

If you enjoyed, "For Such a Time as This? I would love to hear from you: Dawndensmore@gmail.com

For more inspiring information
visit:www.GodsAmazingWays.com

Other books written by Dawn Densmore-Parent:

DIVINE ENCOUNTERS: The Reality of God, Angels and Demons
Experiencing God's Amazing Ways
Experiencing God's Precious, Priceless Promises
For Such A Time As This?

To order this book visit: Amazon.com or visit Kindle ebooks

www.ingramcontent.com/pod-product-compliance
Lightning Source LLC
Chambersburg PA
CBHW060156050426
42446CB00013B/2855